Instant LESS CSS Preprocessor How-to

Practical, hands-on recipes to write more efficient CSS, with the help of the LESS CSS Preprocessor library

Alex Libby

PUBLISHING

BIRMINGHAM - MUMBAI

Instant LESS CSS Preprocessor How-to

First published: February 2013

Production Reference: 1180213

Published by Packt Publishing Ltd.
Livery Place
35 Livery Street
Birmingham B3 2PB, UK.

ISBN 978-1-78216-376-3

www.packtpub.com

Credits

Author
Alex Libby

Reviewer
Yuxian Eugene Liang

Acquisition Editor
Kartikey Pandey

Commissioning Editor
Maria D'souza

Technical Editor
Ankita Meshram

Project Coordinator
Esha Thakker

Proofreader
Maria Gould

Production Coordinator
Melwyn D'sa

Cover Work
Melwyn D'sa

Cover Image
Aditi Gajjar

About the Author

Alex Libby has plenty of experience in IT support, and he has been involved in supporting end users for the last 15 years in a variety of different environments, and currently works as a Technical Analyst, supporting a medium-sized SharePoint estate for an international parts distributor based in the UK. Although Alex gets to play with different technologies in his day job, his first true love has always been the open source movement, and in particular experimenting with CSS/CSS3 and HTML5. To date, Alex has written three books (one on HTML5 Video, one on SASS CSS, and another on JQuery Tools). *LESS CSS Preprocessor How-to* is his fourth book.

I'd like to thank my family and friends for their help and encouragement, and of course Alexis Sellier for producing such a fantastic library. It's certainly made me look at CSS in a completely new light!

About the Reviewer

Yuxian Eugene Liang is a researcher, author, web developer, and business developer. He enjoys solving difficult problems creatively in the form of implementing web applications using Python/Django/Tornado, and JavaScript/Jquery/Node.js. He also enjoys doing research related to the areas of social network analysis, social computing, recommendation algorithms, link analysis, data visualization, data mining, information retrieval, business intelligence, and intelligent user interfaces. He previously authored *JavaScript Testing Beginner's Guide*. Find him at `http://www.liangeugene.com`. Support for this book can also be found at `http://wordpressphonegap.liangeugene.com`.

www.PacktPub.com

Support files, eBooks, discount offers and more

You might want to visit www.PacktPub.com for support files and downloads related to your book.

Did you know that Packt offers eBook versions of every book published, with PDF and ePub files available? You can upgrade to the eBook version at www.PacktPub.com and as a print book customer, you are entitled to a discount on the eBook copy. Get in touch with us at service@packtpub.com for more details.

At www.PacktPub.com, you can also read a collection of free technical articles, sign up for a range of free newsletters and receive exclusive discounts and offers on Packt books and eBooks.

http://PacktLib.PacktPub.com

Do you need instant solutions to your IT questions? PacktLib is Packt's online digital book library. Here, you can access, read and search across Packt's entire library of books.

Why Subscribe?

- ▶ Fully searchable across every book published by Packt
- ▶ Copy and paste, print and bookmark content
- ▶ On demand and accessible via web browser

Free Access for Packt account holders

If you have an account with Packt at www.PacktPub.com, you can use this to access PacktLib today and view nine entirely free books. Simply use your login credentials for immediate access.

Table of Contents

Preface

Imagine the scene, if you will...

It's 5:00 pm on a Friday, and you're looking forward to a good weekend with friends, with thoughts on nothing else except finishing what has been a good week. The trouble is, your boss saunters through the office, and says, "I desperately need the buttons on that e-commerce site you've been working on for the last week redone. The client's not happy with the colors that we've use." You groan silently, and resign yourself to another late night. There are 40 buttons, in all kinds of places, and you have to change each one manually!

Sound familiar? I thought so! It's perhaps a little contrived, but with good reason; what if I said you could change all of the buttons' colors in one go, including the ones which have dependent styles, without changing more than maybe a few lines of code? That would only take a few minutes!

You're probably thinking this is impossible. It's not! Welcome to the world of LESS! LESS is a CSS preprocessor, which was created by Alexis Sellier and originally designed to work using Ruby, but which has since been rewritten to use JavaScript. While it may take a little work to fully implement it into a site, it will repay your time in spades. You will be able to make the kind of changes I've mentioned, and more, with the minimum amount of fuss. The more you use it, the more you will want to incorporate it into your projects.

The real beauty of LESS though is that you don't need to download any large files at all, or spend lots of time installing applications. All you need to get started is one file that weighs in at just over 45 KB, which you can include in the same way as you would for any other JavaScript file.

Intrigued? If so, let's get started!

Please note that all of the tasks in this book are based on Windows, as this is the author's preferred platform. Wherever possible, suggestions for equivalents on the Apple Mac and/or Linux platform will be provided.

What this book covers

Throughout this book, we're going to look at a variety of exercises that are designed to help you get accustomed to working with the basics of the LESS CSS preprocessor language. You're probably wondering what we're going to cover, right? No problem! Let me reveal it all!

Installing Less (Must know): We'll kick off with arguably the most important part of the book, how to install support for LESS; as you'll see later, it is really easy!

Precompiling LESS client side (Must know): While LESS will allow you to compile your CSS styles on the fly, there may be occasions where you want to do this before adding the style code to your site. I'll show you an example of how to do this using one of several applications available.

Precompiling LESS server side (Must know): The beauty of LESS is that you can create your CSS shorthand manually and leave the server to turn this into your compiled code automatically. In this recipe we'll see how to do this using LESS.

Compiling back to LESS from CSS (Should know): You've taken over a site and want to use LESS to help with your CSS development work but are thinking, " How do I rework it into the equivalent LESS code?" It's easy! I can use css2less, surely? Sure, you can, but are the results as good as you might expect?

Autorefreshing using watchr (Must know): As you use LESS, you will no doubt need to fine-tune your styles. This may mean having to recompile the LESS file each time. This little trick will update any changes to styles in the browser, as and when you make them to the LESS code.

Using LESS variables (Must know): Now that we have the installation part of LESS out of the way, let's now focus on looking at how LESS works. We begin with creating simple variables that you can then use to define values in much the same way as you might in any programming language.

Using mixins in LESS (Must know): A useful part of LESS is the ability to include properties from one set of rules into another. In this task I'll show you how to achieve this, and build on it, so that your mixins can accept parameters, or even work out which values to show, based on the outcome of one or more conditions.

Parametric mixins in LESS (Must know): Mixins are a valuable part of LESS; they will help you reduce the amount of code you need to type, as you can reuse code from existing projects. This is great, but there will be occasions when you may want to vary values used in your mixins. In this exercise you will see how you can turn your mixins into dynamic ones, by harnessing the power of parameters.

Pattern-matching in LESS (Must know): So far, we will have looked at how you can create mixins and variables to help reduce the amount of code you need to type each time. However, we can take it even further by controlling what shows and when—welcome to the world of pattern-matching in LESS!

Using JavaScript evaluation in LESS (Should know): You can take advantage of the power of JavaScript within LESS. This opens up some real possibilities, such as getting the screen width, or changing text from lower case to upper case. I'll show you some examples of what you can do, as well as show some of the pitfalls of using JavaScript within your LESS files.

Importing files and escaping code in LESS (Must know): Importing CSS styles into a site usually means a lot of round trips to the server but not with LESS; LESS builds up one CSS source, based on any files that it needs to import, which saves on trips to the server.

Using JavaScript operators in LESS (Should know): Normally, you would need to work out each value for each CSS style and it could be a time-consuming process; using LESS, we can get the server to work them out automatically for us, saving a lot of time, particularly if we need to update a value later!

Creating colors with functions in LESS (Should know): We can do similar things with colors using LESS; imagine choosing one color, then using LESS to work out a whole color scheme for us; this recipe will show you how easy it is to do this.

Grouping/nesting styles in LESS (Should know): I'll bet that over time, you've probably had to write a lot of repeated code, particularly for those styles that were inherited, right? You can avoid the need to do this with LESS; this recipe will show you how you can use nested styles to cut down the code you need to write.

Scoping in LESS (Should know): We can also use the power of scoping in LESS. We can override preset variables used in one mixin with another instance of that variable; LESS will work out which one to use, depending on where it has been scoped in the LESS code.

Using LESS with other libraries (Become an expert): The beauty of LESS is that it helps you become more efficient when writing CSS; it works equally well when used in conjunction with other libraries such as Modernizr. In this demo, we will look at using LESS and Modernizr to style a sample web page, which will produce visually acceptable results on a wide range of browsers.

Using pre-built mixin libraries (Become an expert): Once you are more familiar with LESS, there is a whole world of things you could achieve, even if it is purely to help introduce a more modular approach to your code-writing. In this recipe we're going to harness the power of LESS to rework the code for some progress bars, which you can then reuse in your future projects.

What you need for this book

There will be instances where you may need to install software for a particular recipe. We will go through the specifics of each piece of software ahead of any task. In the meantime, you will need the following:

  ▶   An Internet connection for downloading various pieces of software for each chapter

  ▶   A working installation of WordPress for the form demo towards the end of the book

Many of the exercises in this book will follow the same format. I would recommend saving a copy of the following code as a template to help you when you start working on the exercises throughout this book:

```
<!DOCType html>
<html>
  <head>
    <meta http-equiv="content-type" content="text/html; charset=utf-8"
/>
    <link rel="stylesheet/less" type="text/css" href="XXXXXX.less">
    <script type="text/javascript" src="http://cdnjs.cloudflare.com/
ajax/libs/less.js/1.3.1/less.min.js"> </script>
  </head>
<body>
</body>
</html>
```

Who this book is for

This book is great for those who are new to LESS, and are using CSS preprocessors. You should have some experience of using CSS, although this is not critical. I'll take you through how you can use LESS to make your CSS more modular, and provide some examples, which you can either drop in or adapt for future projects

Conventions

In this book, you will find a number of styles of text that distinguish between different kinds of information. Here are some examples of these styles, and an explanation of their meaning.

Code words in text are shown as follows: "We can include other contexts through the use of the include directive."

A block of code is set as follows:

```
@color-button: #d24444;

#formsubmit {
    color:#fff;
    background:@color-button;
    border:1px solid @color-button - #222;
    padding:5px 12px;
}

.error_message {
    .alert;
    margin: 0 0 12px 0;
}
```

When we wish to draw your attention to a particular part of a code block, the relevant lines or items are set in bold:

```
@color-button: #d24444;

#formsubmit {
    color:#fff;
    background:@color-button;
    border:1px solid @color-button - #222;
    padding:5px 12px;
}

.alert() {
    background: red;
    color: white;
    padding:5px 12px;
}

.error_message {
    .alert;
    margin: 0 0 12px 0;
}
```

New terms and **important words** are shown in bold. Words that you see on the screen, in menus or dialog boxes for example, appear in the text like this: "clicking the **Next** button moves you to the next screen".

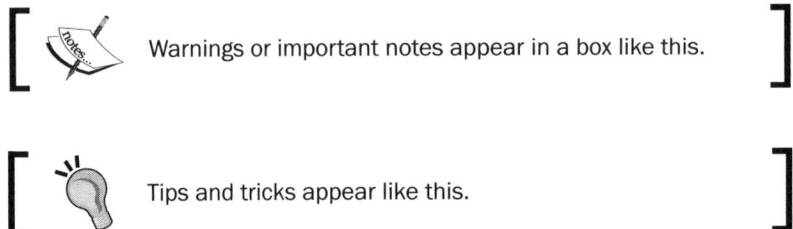

Warnings or important notes appear in a box like this.

Tips and tricks appear like this.

Reader feedback

Feedback from our readers is always welcome. Let us know what you think about this book—what you liked or may have disliked. Reader feedback is important for us to develop titles that you really get the most out of.

To send us general feedback, simply send an e-mail to feedback@packtpub.com, and mention the book title via the subject of your message.

If there is a book that you need and would like to see us publish, please send us a note in the **SUGGEST A TITLE** form on www.packtpub.com or e-mail suggest@packtpub.com.

If there is a topic that you have expertise in and you are interested in either writing or contributing to a book, see our author guide on www.packtpub.com/authors.

Customer support

Now that you are the proud owner of a Packt book, we have a number of things to help you to get the most from your purchase.

Downloading the example code

You can download the example code files for all Packt books you have purchased from your account at http://www.packtpub.com. If you purchased this book elsewhere, you can visit http://www.packtpub.com/support and register to have the files e-mailed directly to you.

Errata

Although we have taken every care to ensure the accuracy of our content, mistakes do happen. If you find a mistake in one of our books—maybe a mistake in the text or the code—we would be grateful if you would report this to us. By doing so, you can save other readers from frustration and help us improve subsequent versions of this book. If you find any errata, please report them by visiting http://www.packtpub.com/submit-errata, selecting your book, clicking on the **errata submission form** link, and entering the details of your errata. Once your errata are verified, your submission will be accepted and the errata will be uploaded on our website, or added to any list of existing errata, under the Errata section of that title. Any existing errata can be viewed by selecting your title from http://www.packtpub.com/support.

Piracy

Piracy of copyright material on the Internet is an ongoing problem across all media. At Packt, we take the protection of our copyright and licenses very seriously. If you come across any illegal copies of our works, in any form, on the Internet, please provide us with the location address or website name immediately so that we can pursue a remedy.

Please contact us at copyright@packtpub.com with a link to the suspected pirated material.

We appreciate your help in protecting our authors, and our ability to bring you valuable content.

Questions

You can contact us at questions@packtpub.com if you are having a problem with any aspect of the book, and we will do our best to address it.

Instant LESS CSS Preprocessor How-to

Welcome to *LESS CSS Preprocessor How-to*, where we take you on a journey through using the LESS library file as a CSS preprocessor language, and show you how the little power of JavaScript can make a positive impact on your CSS development workflow.

Let's start by having a look at how CSS preprocessors work.

Installing LESS (Must know)

We're going to start the recipes in this book by looking at how we can get hold of LESS, and adding support for it to your website. LESS comes in two versions, depending on whether you want to use it client side or server side; for the purpose of this recipe, we're going to use it client side. The library is hosted on Google Code, and can be downloaded or included (as a CDN link) from `http://cdnjs.cloudflare.com/ajax/libs/less.js/1.3.1/less.min.js`.

How to do it...

The following steps will guide you in installing LESS:

1. Let's get started by creating a new folder on your PC, let's call it `test less projects`.

2. Crack open a normal text editor of your choice, save a copy of the code from the *What you need for this book* section in the preface of this book, and save it as `test less include.html`.

3. Add the following in between the `<body>` tags in the code:

```
<form action="">
    Name: <input type="text" class="input" />
    Password: <input type="password" class="input" />
    <input type="submit" value="This is a button" />
</form>
```

4. It shows a very plain, basic form, so let's fix that by starting to use LESS to provide some styling. Create a new document in your text editor, then add the following, and save it as `include.less`:

```
@color-button: #d24444;
#submitfrm {
    color:#fff;
    background:@color-button;
    border:1px solid @color-button - #222;
    padding:5px 12px;
}
```

5. Let's now add a link to this file to your main HTML file, so go ahead and alter your code accordingly:

```
<link rel="stylesheet/less" type="text/css" href="include.less">
```

6. That's all that's required, so if you now open your browser, and view the file, you should see on screen the same as the following screenshot:

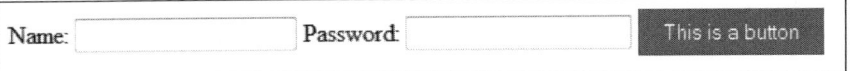

Downloading the example code

You can download the example code files for all Packt books you have purchased from your account at `http://www.packtpub.com`. If you purchased this book elsewhere, you can visit `http://www.packtpub.com/support` and register to have the files e-mailed directly to you.

How it works...

This recipe was intended to serve as a very basic example of how you can use `less.js`. You will be already familiar with what most of the code does, with two exceptions (highlighted in the following code snippet):

```
@color-button: #d24444;
#submitfrm {
    color:#fff;
```

```
    background:@color-button;
    border:1px solid @color-button - #222;
    padding:5px 12px;
}
```

The first exception is simply setting a variable called `color-button`, which holds a value of #d24444; this is the red background you see on the button.

There are a couple of points of interest here:

▸ All variables used in LESS must be preceded with an @ sign, to denote that they are variables

▸ Variables don't actually exist in the LESS library

Huh? I hear you ask. That surely doesn't make sense! Well, let me explain: when using LESS, variables are actually classed as constants, as you can't reassign a new value to an existing predefined variable. There is nothing stopping you from using an existing variable to calculate a new value, but that value must be assigned to a new variable, or used to work out a value for a CSS style:

```
    background:@ color-button;
    border: 1px solid @color-button - #222;
    padding: 5px 12px;
```

The color value calculated for the border then compiles to valid CSS:

```
#submitfrm {
    background: none repeat scroll 0 0 #D24444;
    border: 1px solid #B02222;
    color: #FFFFFF;
    padding: 5px 12px;
}
```

There's more...

In order for the library to work properly, you need to first include links to your `.less` stylesheets, and set the `rel` tag to `stylesheet/less`, in order for them to work properly:

```
<link rel="stylesheet/less" type="text/css" href="styles.less">
```

Note the use of the `rel` attribute on this link, you need to use the `/less` value, in order for LESS to work properly. If you are using HTML5 syntax, you don't need to include the `type="text/less"` and `type="text/javascript"` values.

Next, you need to include LESS; you can either download it from the website and include it locally in the same way that you would include any JavaScript file, or use the following CDN link; in either case, you must include it after your `.less` stylesheet:

```
<script src="http://cdnjs.cloudflare.com/ajax/libs/less.js/1.3.1/less.
min.js"></script>
```

 If you get a 406 error in your browser, you may need to set a MIME (or Internet Media Type, as it is now known), as the `text/LESS` tags may not work properly.

We've seen how LESS can compile styles on the fly, but this may not be ideal if you have a very large site, or have a development process which doesn't allow the use of creating styles dynamically. This isn't an issue with LESS, as you can easily generate the stylesheet prior to including it within your site's pages, as we will see in the next exercise.

Precompiling LESS client side (Must know)

In the previous section, we looked at how you can use Less to dynamically generate your compiled stylesheet from within your site. This may not suit everyone's needs. In this recipe, and the next, we will see some alternatives that allow us to precompile our CSS styles, so we can then include the finished results on our site.

Getting ready

For this recipe we're going to use the open source application WinLESS to compile a LESS file into a normal CSS stylesheet. You can download a copy of the program from `http://www.winless.org`. You will also need your favorite text editor. We're going to create a typical `.less` file; while the format may not make much sense just yet, all will be explained later in this book.

How to do it...

1. Open up the text editor of your choice, and add in the following lines; save it as `testprecompile.less` in the folder you created from the *Installing LESS* section:

    ```
    .border-radius(@radius: 3px) { -webkit-border-radius: @radius;
    -moz-border-radius: @radius; border-radius: @radius; }

    .box-shadow(@x : 2px, @y : 2px, @blur : 5px, @spread : 0, @color :
    rgba(0,0,0,.6)) {
        -webkit-box-shadow: @x @y @blur @spread @color;
        -moz-box-shadow: @x @y @blur @spread @color;
        box-shadow: @x @y @blur @spread @color;
    ```

```
}

div { @color: green; background: @color; width: 300px; height:
300px; margin: 30px auto; .border-radius(10px); .box-shadow(); }
```

2. Double-click on the `WinLess_1.5.3.msi` file you downloaded to install it, accept all defaults, and double-click on it to open the application.

3. Click on the **Add folder** button, and select the folder you created in the first step, and click on **OK** to add it to the folder list of WinLess. Click on the **Refresh folder** button to update the list on the right-hand side as shown in the following screenshot:

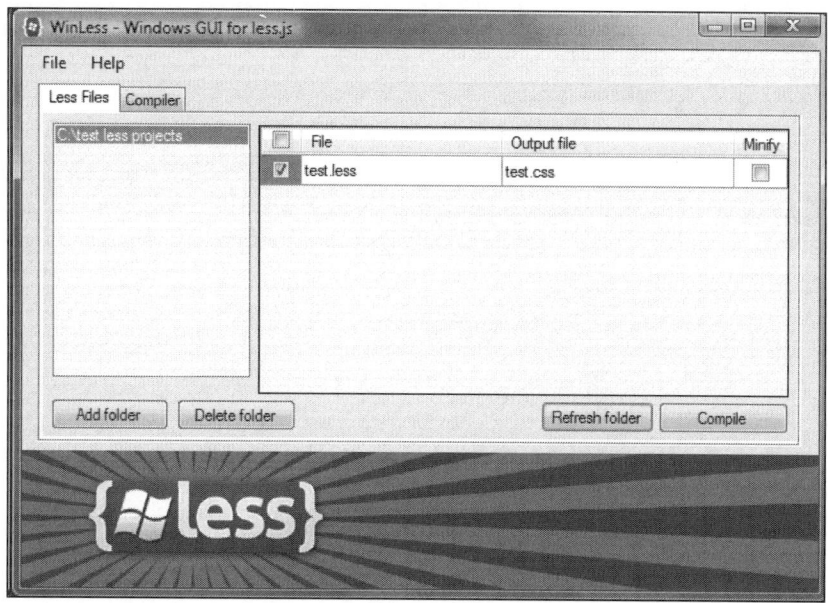

4. Click on **Compile** to generate the CSS file; if you open the resulting CSS file, you will see the generated code as follows:

```
div {
    background: #008000;
    width: 300px;
    height: 300px;
    margin: 30px auto;
    -webkit-border-radius: 10px;
    -moz-border-radius: 10px;
    border-radius: 10px;
    -webkit-box-shadow: 2px 2px 5px 0 rgba(0, 0, 0, 0.6);
    -moz-box-shadow: 2px 2px 5px 0 rgba(0, 0, 0, 0.6);
    box-shadow: 2px 2px 5px 0 rgba(0, 0, 0, 0.6);
}
```

5. As you make further changes to the `.less` file, WinLess will automatically update the CSS file for you; it will remain in the same folder as the `.less` file, until you are ready to use it in a production environment.

How it works...

WinLess is GUI front-ends to the command-line version of LESS, `lessc.cmd`. The GUI takes the content of the `.less` file, parses it, and gives a `.css` file as the output with the compiled CSS styles. WinLess includes an option to maintain a list of files that it will automatically monitor, so that when any are changed, it will automatically update the contents of the equivalent CSS file with the appropriate changes.

There's more...

A number of people have used `lessc.cmd` to create GUI front-ends to help simplify the compilation process. They are available either as open source applications, or on a commercial license, and for a mix of different platforms.

SimpLESS

If you don't need all of the bells and whistles of WinLESS, then you may prefer to use the open source application SimpLESS, which is available for Windows, Linux, or Mac OSX, from `http://wearekiss.com/simpless`. SimpLESS is designed to be run from the system tray, and will automatically generate or update any CSS file silently, without prompting. If you prefer, you can also drag-and-drop files into the application manually as shown in the following screenshot:

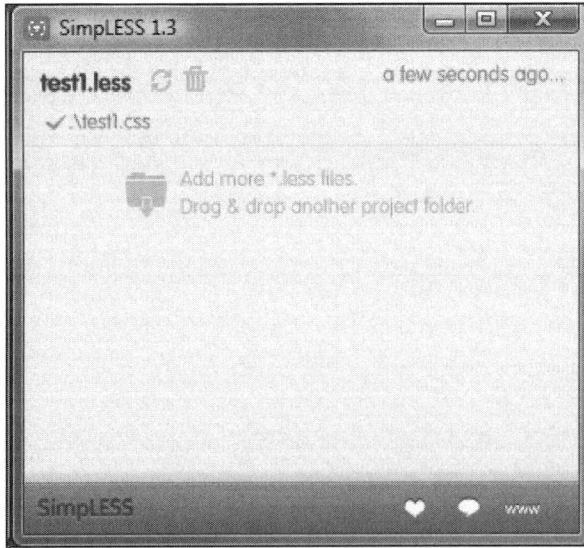

LESS Parser

If you need an application which can work across different platforms independently, you may want to try LESS Parser, which is available at `http://www.proving-ground.be/less/`. This was developed using Adobe Air for Windows 7 but should work on any platform that supports Adobe Air. It's still in development, so there may be some bugs when using on a non-Windows platform:

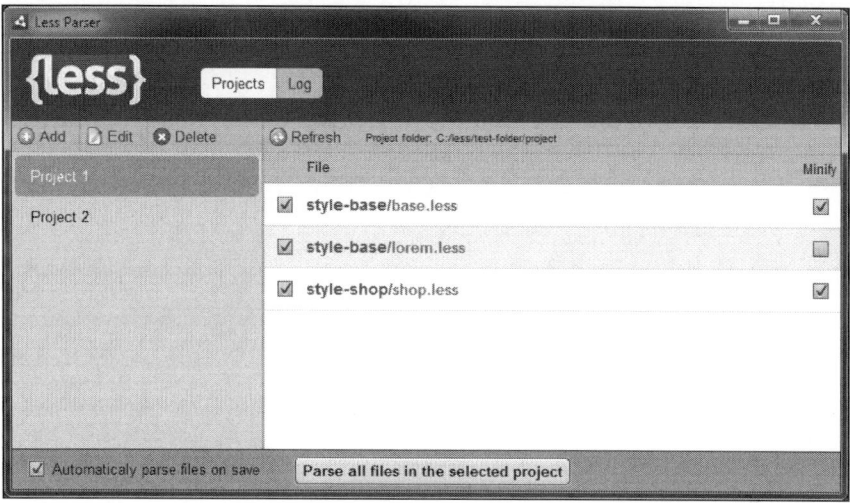

Crunch!

Another application that works in a similar manner is Crunch!. This is an open source software, and available from `http://www.crunchapp.net`. This will watch which folders you select, as well as edit both the source `.LESS` and compiled `.css` files within the same application:

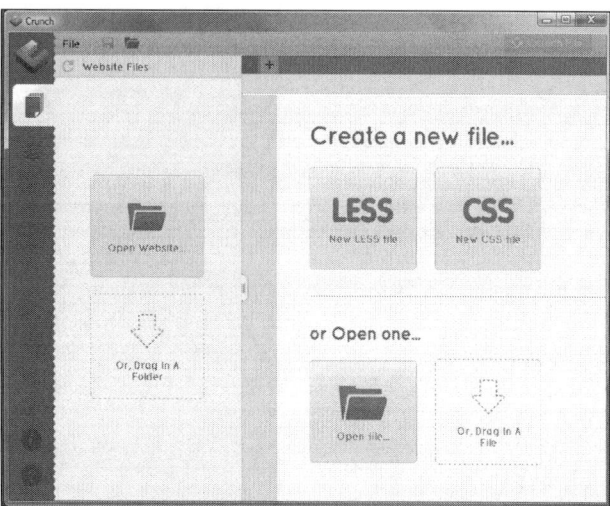

Other alternatives

If you prefer, you can use an online converter, which will achieve the same result, such as the one available at `http://winless.org/online-less-compiler`.

You may also prefer to compile your code on server side; this will be particularly useful if you have an existing development process, and don't want to introduce yet another application into your workflow mix. Let's now take a look at how you can compile your Less code using a server-side based process as part of the next task.

Precompiling LESS server side (Must know)

In this task, we're going to use `Node.js`, which we will hook into a normal text editor. For the purpose of this exercise, we'll use Notepad++, although a similar process will work for other text editors.

Getting ready

For this recipe you will need to avail yourself of a copy of `Node.js`, which is available at `http://nodejs.org`. Make sure you choose a version suitable for your platform; for Windows, this is `node-v0.8.10-x86.msi` at the time of writing. You will also need a copy of Notepad++, a free Windows-based application which you can download from `http://notepad-plus-plus.org`.

How to do it...

1. Let's start by downloading and installing Notepad++ and `Node.js`, accepting all defaults.

2. The Node installer will confirm when it has been completed; at this point, start a command prompt (or equivalent, if not using Windows), and type in `node` to verify that Node has been correctly installed. You will see an error message if this is not the case; a reboot of your PC will usually resolve this fault.

3. Once `Node.js` is installed, go ahead and create a folder to store the `Node.js` LESS module. For the purpose of this exercise I will assume that you have created one at the root of `C:` drive, called `nodejs`.

4. Start a command prompt (note that you must do this as a user with admin rights), and change to the folder you've just created, and type in `npm install less`, as shown in the following screenshot:

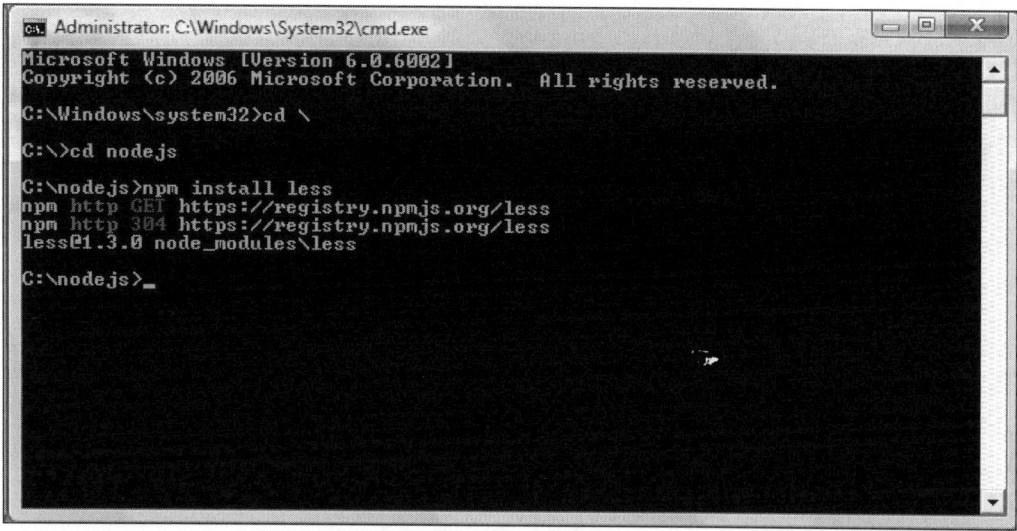

5. Go ahead and open Notepad++ and create a `simple` `.LESS` file. You may need to change the ANSI type to avoid any syntax errors, it is usually set by default.

6. Open the **Run...** dialog box, by clicking on **Run** in the menu, then **Run**:

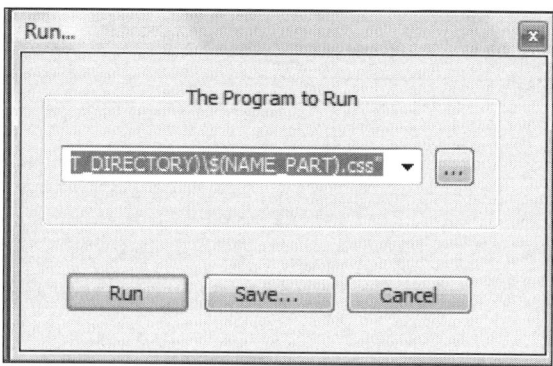

7. Enter the following in the **Run...** dialog box, as shown:

    ```
    "C:\nodejs\node_modules\.bin\lessc.cmd" -x "$(FULL_CURRENT_PATH)"
    > "$(CURRENT_DIRECTORY)\$(NAME_PART).css"
    ```

8. Click on the **Save** button to save the command and enter a descriptive name, such as `LESS Compile`.

9. Select the key combination of your choice. In this instance, I will assume you have used *Alt + F12*; close the dialog box.

10. Open up your LESS file that we used in the *Precompiling LESS client side* section and press *Ctrl + F12*; if you have set it up correctly, you should see a `.css` file appear in the `C:\nodejs` folder you created earlier in this exercise.

How it works...

It's important to note that Notepad++ is not a compiler in the same way that applications such as Visual Studio are; this means we have to tell it which compiler to use, as well as how to compile the file.

The command we've used in the previous exercise can be broken down into several sections as follows:

- ▶ `$(FULL_CURRENT_PATH)`: This gets the full path and filename of the file being worked on in Notepad++
- ▶ `$(CURRENT_DIRECTORY)`: This gets the full path of the current directory; in this instance it will be of the `.less` file being worked on
- ▶ `$(NAME_PART)`: This strips off the path and file extension, to leave the filename

In addition, we've included the `-x` switch for `lessc.cmd`; this tells the `lessc` file to output minified CSS. If you prefer, you can also use the YUI Compressor, by replacing the `-x` option with `-yui-compress`. Any of these options could easily be put into a .BAT, CMD, or .NET application to make it easier to use.

Now that we've seen how to compile your Less code into valid CSS, it should be time to move on and turn our attention to writing some Less code, right? But what if you've seen some CSS code and want to know how it would look if written using Less? Well, you can! I'll show you how in the next exercise.

Compiling back to LESS from CSS (Should know)

In this recipe we're going to see how you can create Less code, based on an existing CSS stylesheet.

Getting ready

For this exercise, all you need is your browser. This will need to be the latest version, as this exercise will not work in some browsers, such as IE8 or below. For the purpose of this exercise, I will assume you are using the latest version of Firefox.

How to do it...

1. Let's start by browsing to `css2less.cc`, and remove all of the code shown in the CSS half of the window. The Less window will automatically update itself when you make any changes.

2. In the left-hand side window, add the following CSS code:

   ```
   #div { color: blue; }

   #div #title { background: #d24444; }
   ```

3. Notice how the contents of the Less section have changed as shown in the following screenshot:

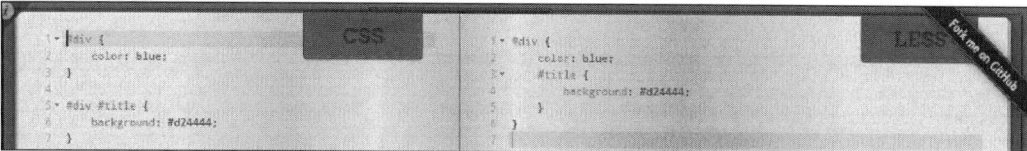

How it works...

The site was designed around the `css2less` script written in Ruby by Marcin Kulik, and which has since been refactored and converted to gem format by Thomas Pierson. The script used on this site is actually very small; it reads in the contents of the existing CSS file (or, in this instance, the contents of the CSS window on the right-hand side of the screen), then creates a new instance of the `Css2Less::Convertor` class, and parses the content with the results appearing on screen almost instantaneously.

There's more...

While this is a great way to learn how to convert CSS styles to their Less equivalents, it is not perfect. There is one drawback you need to be aware of: there is a limit on the number of characters (set at 50,000) that can be converted; the conversion process doesn't work so well on larger or more complex files. For example, if you try converting back the 2600+ lines for Wordpress' Twenty Eleven theme, it will most likely fail!

You will find that there is a limit in what the `less2css.cc` site can manage. It works best on styles that could be nested, but not on styles that could use mixins or variables to help reduce the code. It's a good tool to use when starting out, but you will probably find yourself moving away from using it once you become more accustomed to spotting where Less can help reduce code.

There is one area left for us to look at before we start to write some Less code. If we make a change to our Less code, you would naturally need to refresh the page; in some instances this may not always work correctly, as we will see in the next exercise.

Autorefreshing styles using watchr (Must know)

In this exercise we're going to take a look at a simple, but useful feature called watchr. This allows us to make changes to any less file while still in development, and for us to reload the page without having to force a complete reload of the page from the server.

 Note that this exercise will be in two parts; the first part will be to make the changes to your LESS/HTML code, and the second part will be to preview the changes in your browser.

Getting ready

For this exercise you will need to avail yourself of a copy of your code from the *Installing LESS* section, as well as a normal text editor of your choice.

For the second part of this exercise, if you want to use a local web server to preview your result, you will need to download and install an appropriate web server such as WAMPServer for Windows, available at `http://www.wampserver.com/en`. There will be similar products available for Mac (such as MAMPServer) and Linux users. It is best to try several, and remain with whichever you find easiest to use. For the purpose of this task, I will assume that you have downloaded and installed WAMPServer. If your settings are different, then please alter them accordingly.

How to do it...

1. Let's begin by opening up a copy of the code from the *Installing LESS* section. Immediately below the call to the LESS library, insert the following:

    ```
    <script type="text/javascript" src="http://cdnjs.cloudflare.com/
    ajax/libs/less.js/1.3.1/less.min.js">
    </script>
    <script type="text/javascript">
      less.env = "development";
      less.watch();
      </script>
    </head>
    ```

2. To test it, you need to fire up your local web server, and then save a copy of the HTML and LESS files from the first task into the server's www folder; for WAMPServer, this is normally c:\wamp\www.

3. To preview the changes let's browse to your HTML file from within the server. You need to enter the appropriate URL into your browser, which will be something like this:

   http://127.0.0.1/less/Chapter%201/test%20Less%20include.html

   If all is well, you should not see any changes yet.

4. The change comes when changing the LESS code. Go ahead and change the hex code for the @color-button value, as follows:

```
@color-button: #457668;
#submit {
    color:#fff;
    background:@color-button;
    border:1px solid @color-button - #222;
    padding:5px 12px;
}
```

5. Now go to your browser and alter the URL, so it looks something like this:

   http://127.0.0.1/less/Chapter%201/test%20Less%20include.
   html#!watch

6. Press *Enter* to reload the page. You should see the color change from the original red to a dark green as shown in the following screenshot:

Name:		Password:		This is a button

How it works...

When working with LESS, you will find that compiled styles are stored in the localStorage area of the browser, and that they remain there until the localStorage area is cleared. This means you will have to force a refresh from the server in order to view any changes.

To get around this, you can force the browser into a development mode, which prevents the browser from caching the generated CSS files. The addition of !#watch at the end of the URL then acts as a trigger; it forces the browser to update the generated CSS style, without you having to force a refresh from the server.

 Note that in some instances, you may find this doesn't work when using Google Chrome; Chrome doesn't load local files from the PC's filesystem by default, due to a known issue with loading JavaScript files.

It's time for us to now get stuck into writing some LESS code. Over the next few recipes, we're going to turn our focus to looking at the constituent elements of the Less library, beginning with using Less variables.

Using LESS variables (Must know)

In this exercise we're going to focus on how you can use variables to assign values, which can be reused by LESS throughout the stylesheet. We'll use a simple example of three blocks, using three different colors that will have been chosen based on calculated values, using operator functionality of LESS; we will explore more of this later in this book.

Getting ready

For this exercise you will only need your text editor. As the accompanying LESS code is very small, we will get LESS to compile it on the fly.

How to do it...

1. Remember that template we created at the start of this chapter? Open it in your usual text editor, add the following lines, and save it as `test less variables. html`:

```
<body>
    <div id="div1">This is test number 1</div>
    <div id="div2">This is test number 2</div>
    <div id="div3">This is test number 3</div>
</body>
```

2. Create a second new blank document, and save this as `variables.less`; add in the following lines:

```
@red: #610000;
@light_red: @red + #333;
@dark_red: @red - #333;
@header-font: 'Cookie', cursive;
@header-font-color: #fff;

#div1 { background-color: @dark_red; width: 300px; height:
100px; font-family: @header-font; font-size: 30px; color:
@header-font-color; }

#div2 { background-color: @red; width: 300px; height: 100px;
    font-family: @header-font; font-size: 30px; color: @header-
font-color;  }
```

```
#div3 { background-color: @light_red; width: 300px; height:
100px; font-family: @header-font; font-size: 30px; color:
@header-font-color; }
```

3. If you preview the `test less variables.html` file in your browser, you will see three blocks, with different shades of red; the bottom two are using calculated values that have been subtracted from the original `@red` value:

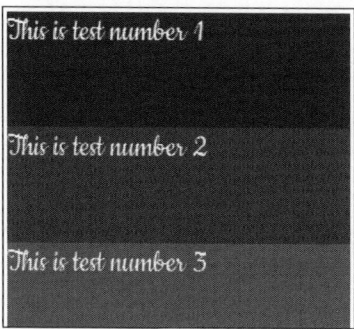

How it works...

In this LESS code we have two parts of LESS' functionality at play here—variables and operators. The former works on a direct swap. We assign a value to a variable, in a similar fashion in many other programming languages, and get LESS to replace any instance of that variable with the appropriate value throughout the code.

The latter uses a similar process, but goes one further. It replaces each instance of a specific variable with its appropriate value, and then works out the calculation. The value rendered on screen will be the result of that calculation. We will look at operator functionality of LESS in the *Using JavaScript operators in LESS* recipe, later in this book.

To see the rendered CSS in action, you can use something like Firebug to view the rendered code, which will look something like the following:

```
#div1 {
  background-color: #2e0000;
  width: 300px;
  height: 100px;
  font-family: 'Cookie', cursive;
  font-size: 30px;
  color: #ffffff;
}

#div2 {
  background-color: #610000;
```

```
    width: 300px;
    height: 100px;
    font-family: 'Cookie', cursive;
    font-size: 30px;
    color: #ffffff;
}

#div3 {
    background-color: #943333;
    width: 300px;
    height: 100px;
    font-family: 'Cookie', cursive;
    font-size: 30px;
    color: #ffffff;
}
```

There's more...

The preceding example was designed to illustrate how variables can be used. If we take the concept a little further, variables can really come into their own in the following scenario.

How many times have you found yourself setting up a specific color scheme for your site, only to find you want to change it halfway through development?

When you first started developing websites, you probably did something like this: you used comments at the start of the CSS stylesheet to specify which colors would be used, right? I bet it was something like the following:

```
/* Colors for my Website
    #ff9900 - Orange - used for links and highlighted items
    #cccccc - Light Gray - used for borders
    #333333 - Dark Black - Used for dark backgrounds and heading text
color
    #454545 - Mid Black - Used for general text color
*/
body { background: #333333; color: #454545; }
a { color:#ff9900; }
h1, h2, h3, h4, h5, h6 { color: #333333; }
```

It works, so you're probably thinking why would I want to change it, correct? There are three good reasons to do so:

- If you decide halfway through developing the site that it's not going to be easy to update each reference, if you have a very large stylesheet.

- Unless you have a very good memory, you may find it hard to remember what each color value is, without having to resort to HTML color names.

- At present, the comments don't really serve any purpose, other than as documentation. What if we could actually use this documentation as part of the styles?

With LESS, we can alter our workflow, and use the documentation as part of the CSS styles:

```
/* Colors for my Website */
@color-orange: #ff9900;
@color-gray_light: #cccccc;
@color-black_dark: #333333;
@color-black_medium: #454545;

body { background: @color-black_dark; color: @color-  black_medium; }
a { color: @color-orange; }
h1, h2, h3, h4, h5, h6 { color: @color-black_dark; }
```

The beauty of using variables here is that you can use more memorable names, which could potentially refer to their location at the same time, such as `@black-top-border`. You can then specify all of the values in a variable block at the beginning of the CSS stylesheet. These could even be hived off into a separate LESS file and imported (more on this later). You could even put comments against each color variable if you desire, depending on how careful you've been with naming each variable!

Using mixins in LESS (Must know)

So far we've looked at creating variables in Less. It is time to take things up a notch, and take a look at a key part of Less functionality: **mixins**.

What are mixins? Put simply, mixins are preset blocks of CSS that you can literally *mix-in* (pun intended!) to produce new CSS styles. They are very much like the building blocks needed to build a house. On their own, they may not be very useful, but once combined into another style, they can become very useful. In this exercise we're going to look at a very simple example of three different colored blocks, for which we will create a **box-shadow mixin** to use in our style code.

For this recipe all you will need is a text editor of your choice.

1. Open up your normal text editor, and save a copy of the template file from the previous recipe as `test less mixins.html`. Add in the following highlighted lines:

```
<body>
   <div class="left_box">Lighter</div>
   <p>
   <div class="middle_box">Original</div>
   <p>
   <div class="right_box">Darker</div>
</body>
```

2. Create a new document in your text editor, and save it as `mixins.less`. You will need to update your HTML code as follows:

```
<link rel="stylesheet/less" type="text/css" href="mixins.less">
```

3. In your LESS file, add in the following styles. We'll break it down into a number of sections, starting with the setting of basic values:

```
@boxwidth: 100px;
@boxheight: 50px;
```

4. We need to add the styles that will determine how the background will be styled, and which control the DIV box sizes:

```
body { font-family: 'Cookie', cursive; font-size: 26px; color:
#ffc; }

div { height: @boxheight; width: @boxwidth; }
```

5. Let's now add in the individual styles for each of the three squares:

```
.left_box { background-color: #FF1010; .box-shadows; }
.middle_box { background-color: #800000; .box-shadows; }
.right_box { background-color: #000000; .box-shadows; }
```

6. The observant among you will have noticed the call for `.box-shadow`, but that we've not set the style for this; let's go ahead and fix that by adding in the following lines:

```
.box-shadows {
  -webkit-box-shadow: 3px 2px 3px rgba(50, 50, 50, 0.75);
  -moz-box-shadow:    3px 2px 3px rgba(50, 50, 50, 0.75);
  box-shadow:         3px 2px 3px rgba(50, 50, 50, 0.75);
}
```

7. If all is well, you will see the following screenshot when previewing the result in your browser:

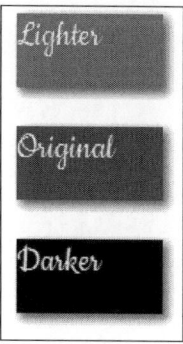

How it works...

Mixins in Less work on a simple principle of replacing code wherever it sees the corresponding CSS style. It is perhaps easier to think of it as a placeholder, or a shorthand code; as soon as Less sees one, it will replace it with the appropriate styles. So, in our example, the `right_box` styles contained this within the LESS code:

```
.right_box {
  background-color: #000000;
  .box-shadows;
}
```

When compiled, LESS will automatically replace it with the following CSS:

```
background-color: black;
-webkit-box-shadow: 3px 2px 3px rgba(50, 50, 50, 0.75);
-moz-box-shadow: 3px 2px 3px rgba(50, 50, 50, 0.75);
box-shadow: 3px 2px 3px rgba(50, 50, 50, 0.75);
```

The browsers will then discard the box-shadow style it doesn't understand; in this instance, this is what would be left when looking at this demo from within Firefox:

```
.right_box {
  background-color: #000000;
  box-shadow: 3px 2px 3px rgba(50, 50, 50, 0.75);
}
```

Although we've looked at a simple example here, the same principle works for a multitude of uses. There really is no limit in what you can achieve, provided you plan your styles carefully!

The downside of using mixins is that there will be instances where you have styles that are very similar to existing ones, but which you can't alter to fit them, as one or more of the values has to remain unique. As you can see from the preceding example, the box-shadow values are fixed for all three boxes, with only the browser showing the relevant box-shadow style attribute, depending on which browser you use.

Now you're probably thinking that this is a bit irritating, as you can't vary the styles, and that it will likely mean that you will still have some duplication that you can't remove. What if I said that it was possible to pass different parameters to mixins, in much the same way as you would do with functions in PHP, for example? Well, you can, and we'll have a look at how to do this within the next recipe.

Parametric mixins in LESS (Must know)

In the previous recipe, we focused on how we could reuse blocks of code, as mixins, into subsequent styles, thereby saving code when writing. This is very useful but I hear you ask, what about those similar styles we can't rework into our mixin, because there are some slight differences that have to remain—can we do any better?

Yes we can with the use of parameter functionality within our blocks of code. In this exercise we're going to adapt the code from the previous exercise, so it uses parameters to show the same three boxes.

Getting ready

For this exercise all we need is our text editor, and a copy of the template file we created at the start of this chapter.

How to do it...

1. Open up your normal text editor, and save a copy of the template file you used earlier as `test less parametric mixins.html`. Add in the following highlighted lines:

```
<body>
    <div class="left_box">Lighter</div>
    <p>
    <div class="middle_box">Original</div>
    <p>
    <div class="right_box">Darker</div>
</body>
```

2. Create a new document in your text editor, and save it as `parametricmixins.less`. You will need to update your HTML code as follows:

```
<link rel="stylesheet/less" type="text/css"
href="parametricmixins.less">
```

3. In your LESS file, add in the following styles. We'll break it down into a number of sections, starting with the setting of basic values:

```
@boxwidth: 100px;
@boxheight: 50px;
```

4. We need to add the styles that will determine how the background will be styled and control the DIV box sizes:

```
body { font-family: 'Cookie', cursive; font-size: 26px;
    color: #ffc; }

div { height: @boxheight; width: @boxwidth; }
```

5. Let's now add in the individual styles for each of the three squares shown on screen:

```
.left_box { background-color: #FF1010; .box-shadow(3px 3px    5px,
rgba(50, 50, 50, 0.75)); }

.middle_box { background-color: #800000; .box-shadow(3px 3px
5px, rgba(50, 50, 50, 0.75)); }

.right_box { background-color: #000000; .box-shadow(3px 3px    5px,
rgba(50, 50, 50, 0.75)); }
```

6. The observant among you will have noticed the call for `.box-shadow`, but that we've not set the style for this; let's go ahead and fix that by adding in the following lines:

```
.box-shadow(@style, @c) {
        box-shadow:         @style @c;
        -webkit-box-shadow: @style @c;
        -moz-box-shadow:    @style @c;
}
```

7. If all is well, you will see the following screenshot when previewing the result in your browser:

How it works...

When researching for this book, I read many comments from people who had used Less before. One overriding theme was that it brought to CSS what we have had in programming languages for years. This is particularly true when talking about parametric mixins!

The beauty of parametric mixins is that they work in much the same way as normal functions in programming code; you create a base function, into which you can pass values that get substituted and compiled into valid CSS.

The key to this is in the function:

```
.box-shadow(@style, @c) {
    box-shadow:          @style @c;
    -webkit-box-shadow: @style @c;
    -moz-box-shadow:     @style @c;
}
```

Here we have two variables (@style and @c) that are being passed through to the function:

```
.left_box { background-color: #FF1010; .box-shadow(3px 3px      5px,
rgba(50, 50, 50, 0.75)); }
```

So when we call the function, the appropriate values are substituted by Less to produce the following valid CSS:

```
.left_box {
  background-color: #FF1010;
  box-shadow: 3px 3px 5px rgba(50, 50, 50, 0.75);
  -webkit-box-shadow: 3px 3px 5px rgba(50, 50, 50, 0.75);
  -moz-box-shadow: 3px 3px 5px rgba(50, 50, 50, 0.75);
}
```

```
.middle_box {
  background-color: #800000;
  box-shadow: 3px 3px 5px rgba(50, 50, 50, 0.75);
  -webkit-box-shadow: 3px 3px 5px rgba(50, 50, 50, 0.75);
  -moz-box-shadow: 3px 3px 5px rgba(50, 50, 50, 0.75);
}
.right_box {
  background-color: #000000;
  box-shadow: 3px 3px 5px rgba(50, 50, 50, 0.75);
  -webkit-box-shadow: 3px 3px 5px rgba(50, 50, 50, 0.75);
  -moz-box-shadow: 3px 3px 5px rgba(50, 50, 50, 0.75);
}
```

Here, we have three identical function calls within each CSS style; we could take this further by using different values for each function call. It really is a case of the sky is the limit, particularly for an example such as box-shadow. A good way to get started is to use a CSS3 generator (http://css3gen.com/box-shadow/) to create the effect you are looking for, and then use the resulting CSS in the appropriate function call. In all cases, you can pass whatever values are required, while still using the same function in each case. The code will compile and work, as long as they are sensible values!

There's more...

I mentioned earlier that parametric mixins are very similar to functions in code such as PHP; not only can you pass variables to a Less function, but you can also specify static variables in functions that can then be overridden, as well as you can use a special @arguments keyword as a shorthand command. You can even pass parametric mixins without parameters (yes, you read right!). Let's take a look at each of these in turn, beginning with default values.

Default values and multiple parameters

If you often use the same value for at least one of the parameters in your mixin, you can set a default value against one or more of your parameters. This means that if a value is not passed, it will assume that the default value should be used:

```
.box-shadow(@style: 3px 3px 5px, @c) {
    box-shadow:            @style @c;
    -webkit-box-shadow: @style @c;
    -moz-box-shadow:      @style @c;
}


.left_box {
background-color: #FF1010;
.box-shadow(10px 3px 5px, rgba(50, 50, 50, 0.75));
}
```

```
.right_box { background-color: #FF1010; .box-shadow(3px 3px    5px,
rgba(50, 50, 50, 0.75)); }
```

In the preceding example, we're passing the default value of 10px 3px 5px for the `@style` variable in the `.left_box` style; this will override the existing style set to produce the following:

```
.left_box {
  background-color: #FF1010;
  box-shadow: 10px 3px 5px rgba(50, 50, 50, 0.75);
  -webkit-box-shadow: 10px 3px 5px rgba(50, 50, 50, 0.75);
  -moz-box-shadow: 10px 3px 5px rgba(50, 50, 50, 0.75);
}
.right_box {
  background-color: #FF1010;
  box-shadow: 3px 3px 5px rgba(50, 50, 50, 0.75);
  -webkit-box-shadow: 3px 3px 5px rgba(50, 50, 50, 0.75);
  -moz-box-shadow: 3px 3px 5px rgba(50, 50, 50, 0.75);
}
```

Using all arguments at once

A useful trick when using parametric mixins is the ability to simply include all of the parameters at once without changing them. To do this, you can use the special keyword `@arguments` within your mixin. Let's have a look at how this works.

Imagine you have a style such as the following one:

```
div { border:1px solid #bbb; }
```

It's a fairly ordinary style, a mauveish color border for a DIV. Let's turn this into a parametric mixin:

```
.gray_border(@width: 1px, @type: solid, @color: #bbb){
    border: @width @type @color; }
div { .gray_border(2px, dashed); }
```

While it may initially look odd, it does compile into valid CSS:

```
div { border: 2px dashed #bbbbbb; }
```

So far so good. I don't know about you though, but to me that looks slightly clumsy. Granted, it does work, but we can do better than this. In place of the three keywords used on the border attribute, let's use the `@arguments` keyword here:

```
.gray_border(@width: 1px, @type: solid, @color: #bbb){
    border: @arguments; }
div { .gray_border(2px, dashed); }
```

Doesn't this look better? It will still compile to valid CSS, but removes the clumsy looking three attributes used before, and replaces it with a single one. The `@arguments` keyword outputs all of the variables assigned in the call, one after another, to produce this:

```
div { border:2px dashed #bbbbbb; }
```

There is trouble here; what happens if you want to use mixins to help group your styles, but didn't want to show it in the compiled output? No problem! We don't always have to use parameters within parametric mixins; leaving the parameters completely blank will also work.

Parametric mixins without parameters

When you start using mixins, you will find that there will be instances when you want to use a mixin to help reduce the code in your LESS file, but which doesn't need to act directly on any element or selector within your website. It would be great, therefore, if you could set it so that LESS didn't show it as part of the compiled output. This is very easy to do; let's take a look at how to do it.

Imagine you have two styles, where `.alert` is the mixin, and `.error_message` is the style using that mixin:

```
.alert { background: red; color: white; padding: 5px 12px; }
.error_message { .alert; margin: 0 0 12px 0; }
```

Normally, when compiled, it would show the following CSS styles, which are perfectly valid, but the CSS would include the mixin style, which we don't necessarily need to include:

```
.alert { background: red; color: white; padding:5px 12px; }
.error_message { background: red; color: white; padding:5px 12px;
margin: 0 0 12px 0; }
```

We now add `()` after the initial style name as follows:

```
.alert() {
    background: red;
    color: white;
    padding:5px 12px;
}
.error_message { .alert; margin: 0 0 12px 0; }
```

We will get the following CSS:

```
.error_message { background: red; color: white; padding:5px   12px;
margin: 0 0 12px 0; }
```

Using this method means that you can build up a number of mixins throughout your LESS file, and set LESS to incorporate those styles where appropriate, without including the original mixin styles.

Pattern-matching in LESS (Must know)

In the previous section we focused on how you can use variables to help build up reusable blocks of code, or mixins, but what if you could control which styles are used and when? Huh? You're probably thinking that CSS can do this already, at least in the part where you can define which styles are used. After all, this is standard functionality, right?

Sure it's standard, but not the ability to determine that if say color A is used, then color B should be used, and not color C. This is where you can use Less to create guarded mixins. In this exercise we're going to show a number of squares on screen, where the background color is being determined dynamically, based on how light or dark the color has been set on one of squares.

Getting ready

For this exercise all we need is our text editor, and a copy of the template file we created at the start of this chapter.

How to do it...

1. Open up your normal text editor, and save a copy of the template file we created earlier at the start of the chapter as `test less guarded mixins.html`. Add the following highlighted lines:

    ```
    <body>
        <div class="left_box">Lighter</div>
        <p>
        <div class="middle_box">Original</div>
        <p>
        <div class="right_box">Darker</div>
    </body>
    ```

2. Create a new document in your text editor, and save it as `test less guarded mixins.css` and then add the following line to your HTML code:

    ```
    <link rel="stylesheet/less" type="text/css" href="test less
    guarded mixins.less">
    ```

3. In your LESS file, add the following styles. We'll break it down into a number of sections, starting with the setting of basic values, and the control statement to determine which background color we're going to use:

    ```
    @boxwidth: 100px;
    @boxheight: 50px;

    .set-bg-color (@text-color) when (lightness(@text-color) >= 50%) {
    background-color: #fff; }
    ```

```
.set-bg-color (@text-color) when (lightness(@text-color) < 50%) {
background-color: #ccc; }
```

4. We need to add the styles that will determine how the background will be styled, and which control the DIV box sizes:

```
body { font-family: 'Cookie', cursive; font-size: 26px;
    color: #ffc; .set-bg-color(#FF1010); }


div { height: @boxheight; width: @boxwidth; }
```

5. Let's now add in the individual styles for each of the three squares shown on screen:

```
.left_box { background-color: #FF1010; .box-shadow(3px 3px    5px,
rgba(50, 50, 50, 0.75)); }


.middle_box { background-color: #800000; .box-shadow(3px 3px
5px, rgba(50, 50, 50, 0.75)); }


.right_box { background-color: #000000; .box-shadow(3px 3px    5px,
rgba(50, 50, 50, 0.75)); }
```

6. The observant among you will have noticed the call for .box-shadow, but that we've not set the style for this; let's go ahead and fix that by adding the following lines:

```
.box-shadow(@style, @c) when (iscolor(@c)) {
    box-shadow:         @style @c;
    -webkit-box-shadow: @style @c;
    -moz-box-shadow:    @style @c;
}
```

7. If all is well, you will see the following when previewing the result in your browser:

How it works...

The key behind guarded mixins is that they only take effect if a particular condition is true. A good example is controlling the color used on the background of a page. If you have elements on page that use a light color, you would most likely want a dark color, and certainly not white! Equally, the converse is true; if your elements are dark in color, you may well want a light (or even white) color background.

Let's take a look at an example:

```
.set-bg-color (@text-color) when (lightness(@text-color) >= 50%) {
background-color: #fff; }
.set-bg-color (@text-color) when (lightness(@text-color) < 50%) {
background-color: #ccc; }
```

Here we've set the `.set-bg-color` property to be either gray or white, depending on whether the `@text-color` variable is either a light (that is, lower than 50 percent), or a dark (greater than 50 percent) color. When compiled, you will get the correct background, based on whatever value has been set for `@text-color`:

```
.box-1 { color: #BADA55; .set-bg-color(#BADA55); }
```

There's more...

Although this recipe was designed to be overly simple, you can do some fancy things with it, such as recursion, where LESS can call itself with an updated value creating a loop. You're probably thinking: where can I use that? Easy! Did you ever have to build a number of identical icons, which all use similar CSS? How about building them into a sprite, then using LESS to generate the CSS for you, using a loop? The styles will all have the same text prefix, such as `.myclass1`, `.myclass2`, and so on, but it's a small price to pay if it can save you a heap of work, as long as you use a sensible prefix!

 If you want to see the example code on how to do this, take a look at the following post:

`http://blog.thehippo.de/2012/04/programming/do-a-loop-with-less-css/`

Using JavaScript evaluation in LESS (Should know)

A powerful feature within Less is the ability to use basic JavaScript to generate CSS, such as using the `screen.height` function to determine how big your visitor's screen is. In this exercise we're going to demonstrate the power of using JavaScript within Less to draw a simple shape on screen, which uses the `screen.height` function of JavaScript.

Getting ready

For this exercise all we need is your text editor.

How to do it...

1. We'll begin with opening a copy of the template we created at the start of this chapter; add the following lines, and save it as `test Less javascript evaluation.html`:

    ```html
    <body>
       <div id="testbox">This is test number 1</div>
    </body>
    ```

2. Create a new file, add the following lines of code, and save this as `test Less javascript evaluation.less`:

    ```less
    @height: `screen.width`;

    #testbox { background-color: orange; height: 100px; width: ~`@{width}/2 + "px"`; }
    ```

3. Test the HTML file in your browser; you should see something like the following screenshot:

This is test number 1

How it works...

Although this is an overly simplified example, it serves to illustrate how you can use JavaScript to determine how big the box should appear. The use of LESS code is based around standard JavaScript code, but must use the ~`...` format to ensure that it is correctly interpreted by the compiler:

```less
#testbox {
  background-color: orange;
  height: 100px;
  width: 640px;
}
```

 Note that using JavaScript in CSS can produce some very powerful effects; you should take care over using it, as it is open to abuse, and can be a security risk on your site if you are not careful!

Importing files and escaping code in LESS (Must know)

In this recipe we're going to move away for the moment and focus on a couple of important features of Less that you should be aware of: importing Less or CSS files and escaping non-standard code. Let's take a look at importing files first, using the prebuilt `LessElements` mixin, which we will use to create a basic alert that you can use in your projects.

Getting ready

For this recipe, you will need to crank up any normal text editor of your choice and visit `http://www.lesselements.com` to download the prebuilt `Less Elements` mixin library.

How to do it...

1. Let's begin by opening up a text editor of your choice, adding a copy of the template that we created at the start of the chapter, and saving it as `test less import. html`.

2. Now that we have our framework in place, let's go ahead and add in a `<div>` tag, which acts as the basis for our alert:

    ```
    <body>
    <div class="alert">
        <p>Hello World! (or, you know, maybe something a bit more
    pertinent to your site...)</p>
    </div>
    </body>
    ```

3. If you were to look at this in a browser, it's going to look very plain; we can fix that by adding in the CSS; save the following as `test less import.less`:

    ```
    @import "elements.less";

    .alert { background: ~"#fff6bf url(images/exclamation.png)    15px
    center no-repeat"; text-align: left; padding: 10px    20px 10px
    50px; border-top: 2px solid #ffd324; border-  bottom: 2px solid
    #ffd324; .box-shadow(0 1px 2px #999);
      Width: 40%;
    }
    ```

4. Add a link to it from our HTML code:

```
<link rel="stylesheet/less" type="text/css" href="import.less">
```

5. Save your work and preview it in your browser; if all is well, you should see something like the following screenshot:

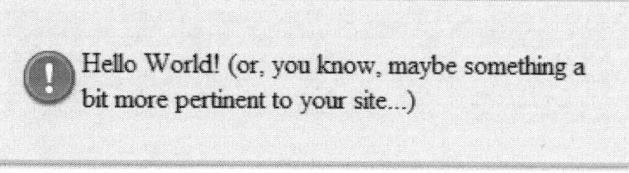

How it works...

Although this is an overly simplified example, it demonstrates perfectly how you can import mixins from established mixin libraries, or even your own, and use them from within your own code. To prove this, have a look at the compiled code from the preceding exercise in something like Firebug; it will show the following code:

```
.alert {
    background: url("images/exclamation.png") no-repeat scroll 15px
center #FFF6BF;
    border-bottom: 2px solid #FFD324;
    border-top: 2px solid #FFD324;
    box-shadow: 0 1px 2px #999999;
    padding: 10px 20px 10px 50px;
    text-align: left;
    width: 40%;
}
```

We'll see more examples of this later in the book.

There's more...

The beauty of LESS is that it will always create a single compiled CSS file, ready for production use. This helps to cut down page load time, as the number of server requests is reduced. You can include any number of LESS files within your main LESS file, allowing you to use a modular approach. Mixins and variables can be separated into separate files for colors, typography, grids, and so on, which you could then reuse in other projects. You can import files using either of the following methods; the .less extension is optional:

```
@import "typography.less";
@import "typography";
```

If you want to import a CSS file and don't want LESS to process it, just use the `.css` extension:

```
@import "typography.css";
```

Let's move on and take a look at another part of LESS functionality using JavaScript operators.

Using JavaScript operators in LESS (Should know)

Remember a previous exercise, where we created a number of squares on screen which were filled in with colors defined by LESS based on a given single color? Well, you can do something similar with text by using JavaScript operators. In this exercise we're going to show a number of headings on screen, which have been styled using operators to determine sizes and colors to be used.

How to do it...

Perform the following steps to get the the server to work out each value for each CSS style automatically:

1. Open a copy of the template you created at the start of this chapter, add the following lines, and save it as `test less operators.html`:

    ```
    <body>
    <h1>Heading 1</h1>
    <h2>Heading 2</h2>
    <h3>Heading 3</h3>
    <h4>Heading 4</h4>
    <h5>Heading 5</h5>
    </body>
    ```

2. Create a new document, add the following lines, and save this as `operators.less`:

    ```
    @mainColour: #631;
    @h1Size: 5em;

    h1 { color: @mainColour; font-size: @h1Size; }

    h2 { color: lighten(@mainColour, 10%); font-size: @h1Size * .8; }

    h3 { color: lighten(@mainColour, 20%); font-size: @h1Size * .6; }

    h4 { color: lighten(@mainColour, 30%); font-size: @h1Size * .4; }

    h5 { color: lighten(@mainColour, 40%); font-size: @h1Size * .2; }
    ```

3. If all is well, you will see the following appear in your browser:

Heading 1
Heading 2
Heading 3
Heading 4
Heading 5

How it works...

In this exercise we've used LESS to set the size and color to be used for each heading. The `font-size` value is worked out by multiplying a set value of 5em by 0.4, 0.6, or 0.8, depending on which heading size is being defined; this gives values of 2em, 3em, and 4em respectively. The color strength is set in a similar fashion, this time using the `lighten` command to progressively lighten the color from 10 percent to 40 percent, depending on which heading style is being defined. The same principle can be applied to other elements, such as buttons; we'll see how to do this in the next recipe.

Creating colors with operators in LESS (Should know)

At the start of the book, we took a look at how you can use variables to assign values in your CSS styling; the observant among you may have spotted something: we were using some basic operators to create colors. In this recipe we're going to extend this principle and use it to style one of the most important components of any website—the humble button! Normally, you would specify styles either using a selector ID or a class. While it will work, it will make things harder when updating or changing styles. Less can really help here; in this exercise we're going to create a base button, using the color function. We'll also look at how to alter the fill-in and border colors used at the same time, by altering the base color.

Getting ready

For this exercise all we need is our text editor.

How to do it...

1. Let's start by opening a copy of the template you created at the start of this chapter, adding the following lines, and saving it as `test less operators.html`:

```
<body>
  <form action="demo_form.php">
    Username: <input type="text" name="usrname" /><br />
    <input type="submit" value="Submit" />
  </form>
</body>
```

2. Open your text editor, create a new document, and add the following lines; save it as `coloroperators.css`:

```
body { padding: 20px; }

@color-button: #d24444;
input.submit { color:#fff; background:@color-button;
border: 1px solid @color-button - #222; padding:5px 12px; }
```

3. If you preview the file in your browser, you will see the following:

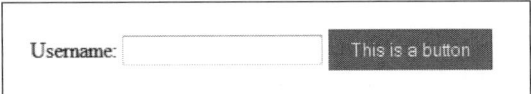

How it works...

In this exercise we've used a simple operator to add or subtract a given number from the HEX code to arrive at the border color. In this instance the border color is #B02222, which gives the button a slightly darker color than that of the main button.

There's more...

The beauty of using variables here is that if you suddenly decide you want to change the color scheme on your site, you only need to change it in one place; all of the borders will be updated at the same time to a suitable shade that fits in with the new color. We can take this a step further and mix in some gradients in the LESS file. This works best if you choose a mid-point color and use this to define your gradient. A good example is to make the start of the gradient lighter and finish on a slightly darker color:

```
body { padding: 20px; }

@color-button: #faa51a;
input.submit {
  @color: #faa51a;
  background: -webkit-gradient(linear, left top, left bottom, from(@
color + #151515), to(@color - #151515));
  background: -moz-linear-gradient(top,  @color + #151515, @color -
#151515);
  border:1px solid @color-button - #222;
  padding:5px 12px;
}
```

This results in a button with a nice looking transition effect as shown in the following screenshot:

Creating colors with functions (Should know)

In this recipe we're going to use the power of LESS to create colored <div> tags, where the colors are chosen dynamically using the chosen base color and a number of functions of LESS.

Getting ready

For this exercise all we need is our text editor.

How to do it...

1. Open a copy of the template that we created at the start of this chapter in your usual text editor, add the following lines, and save it as test less colors.html:

    ```
    <body>
      <div class="left_box"></div>
      Lighter<p>
      <div class="middle_box"></div>
      Original<p>
      <div class="right_box"></div>
      Darker
    </body>
    ```

2. Create a new document, add the following lines, and save this as `colors.less`:

```
@color: #800000;
@boxwidth: 100px;
@boxheight: 50px;

body { font-family: 'Devonshire', cursive; font-size: 24px; }
div { height: @boxheight; width: @boxwidth; }
.left_box { background-color: lighten(@color, 28%); }
.middle_box { background-color: @color; }
.right_box { background-color: darken(@color, 28%); }
```

3. Open the file in your browser. If all is well, you will see the following appear:

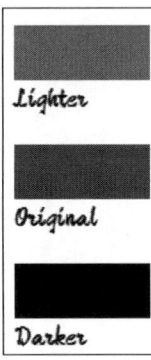

4. We're going to use a different function here, so we need to alter the descriptions shown against each `<div>` tag first, otherwise they won't make sense:

```
<div class="left_box"></div>
Desaturated<p>
<div class="middle_box"></div>
Original<p>
<div class="right_box"></div>
Saturated
</body>
```

5. In this example, we're going to use two new commands—desaturate and saturate—so alter the CSS as follows:

```
.left_box { background-color: desaturate(@color, 28%); }

.right_box { background-color: saturate(@color, 28%); }
```

6. Preview the results in your browser; you will now see a completely different set of colors being used:

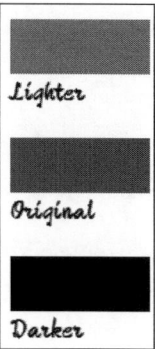

7. We're going to use the `Spin` keyword now, so we need to alter the descriptions so they make sense:

```
<div class="left_box"></div>
Spin -<p>
<div class="middle_box"></div>
Original<p>
<div class="right_box"></div>
Spin +
</body>
```

8. We need to update the styles as shown in the following highlighted lines of code:

```
.left_box {
    background-color: spin(@color, 28%);
}

.right_box {
    background-color: spin(@color, -28%);
}
```

9. If all is well, you should see the same as the following screenshot if you preview the file in your browser:

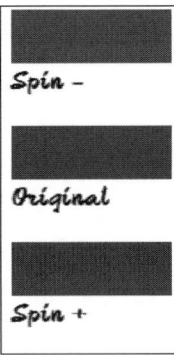

How it works...

Although we've worked with using hex codes for colors throughout the previous two exercises, it is important to note that every color used in LESS is actually converted to an HSL (hue, saturation, lightness) equivalent.

What's the reason for this, I hear you ask? It's simple! Unless you have a hidden talent in being able to speak in HEX, most people find that HEX values don't come naturally to them. While some HEX colors such as #ff0000 are relatively easy to decipher, you'd be hard pressed to know that something such as #1f6b2d would translate as deep green!

The beauty of using HSL means that if you have an existing color, such as #e147d4 (magenta-purple), and wanted a creamier version, then you can easily do this:

```
@color: #e147d4;
@new_color: hsl(hue(@color), 35%, 77%);
```

The new color will maintain the same hue as the existing one, but have a different saturation and brightness; it would be harder to work out the the resulting #c480bf code if you are thinking purely in HEX.

There's more...

You can also use functions within functions when working in LESS. For example, if you wanted to desaturate and spin a color, you can do so by executing the following code:

```
@color: #c480bd;
.class { background-color: desaturate(spin(@color, 18), 12%); }
```

This is great, but it does highlight one small thing though: the similarities in each LESS style. This exercise was deliberately simplified, but if you were to use similar principles to style a number of similar, but more complex items, you could end up with a lot of duplicated code, right? This isn't an issue if you are using LESS; you can group a number of styles together using namespaces, which I will show you how to use in the next recipe.

Grouping/nesting styles in LESS (Should know)

If you regularly develop code, you may well have used namespaces in some form or other. Did you know you could use them in CSS?

That's right! With the power of LESS comes the ability to group CSS styles into logical groups, or namespaces, which you can reuse throughout your code. In the event you need to alter styles on some of the items you are styling, you can do this by adding additional styles that only apply to certain items. Let's take a look and see how this works, using a simple example of styling three buttons from a basic form; this is adapted from a tutorial created by Nick La, at `http://webdesignerwall.com/tutorials/css3-gradient-buttons`.

Getting ready

For this exercise all we need is a text editor. Everything else will be provided within the code.

How to do it...

1. Fire up your normal text editor, save a copy of the template we created at the start of this chapter, and add the following in the `<head>` section:

    ```
    <link rel="stylesheet" type="text/less" href="namespaces.less">
    ```

2. Add the following code and save it as `test less namespaces.html`:

    ```
    <body>
      <form action="demo_form.php">
        Username: <input type="text" name="username" />
        <input type="submit" value="Submit" class="redbutton"/>
      </form>
    ```

```
<p>
<form action="demo_form.php">
  Username: <input type="text" name="username" />
  <input type="submit" value="Submit" class="orangebutton"/>
</form>
<p>
<form action="demo_form.php">
  Username: <input type="text" name="username" />
  <input type="submit" value="Submit" class="bluebutton"/>
</form>
</body>
```

3. Create a new document and save it as `namespaces.less`; there are a lot of LESS styles to add, so let's begin with the base button style:

```
#button_base {
  .button { display: inline-block; margin: 0 2px; outline:
none; cursor: pointer; text-align: center; text-decoration:
none; font: 14px Arial, Helvetica, sans-serif; padding:    .5em 2em
.55em; text-shadow: 0 1px 1px rgba(0,0,0,.3);
    -webkit-border-radius: .5em; -moz-border-radius: .5em;
    border-radius: .5em; -webkit-box-shadow: 0 1px 2px
rgba(0,0,0,.2); -moz-box-shadow: 0 1px 2px rgba(0,0,0,.2);
box-shadow: 0 1px 2px rgba(0,0,0,.2);

    &:hover { text-decoration: underline; }
     &:active { position: relative; top: 1px; }
  }
  .medium { font-size: 12px; padding: .4em 1.5em .42em; }
}
```

4. The next block controls the individual color styling; we begin with creating the base colors and styles:

```
.defined_color (@color1) {
  color: lighten(@color1, 10%);
  border: solid 1px darken(@color1, 27%);
  background: darken(@color1, 13%);
  background: -webkit-gradient(linear, left top, left bottom,
from(darken(@color1, 4%)), to(darken(@color1, 24%)));

  background: -moz-linear-gradient(top,  darken(@color1, 18%),
darken(@color1, 38%));
  filter:  progid:DXImageTransform.Microsoft.
gradient(startColorstr='darken(@color1, 4%)',
endColorstr='darken(@color1, 24%)');
```

5. We need to add some action to show when we hover over buttons, so go ahead and add the following lines of code:

```
&:hover {
    background: darken(@color1, 24%);
    background: -webkit-gradient(linear, left top, left bottom,
from(darken(@color1, 27%)), to(darken(@color1, 17%)));
    background: -moz-linear-gradient(top,  darken(@color1, 27%),
darken(@color1, 17%));
    filter:  progid:DXImageTransform.Microsoft.
gradient(startColorstr='darken(@color1, 27%)',
endColorstr='darken(@color1, 17%)');
    }
```

6. We finish creating the styles by adding in the `:active` pseudo class:

```
&:active {
    color: darken(@color1, 34%);
    background: -webkit-gradient(linear, left top, left bottom,
from(darken(@color1, 24%)), to(darken(@color1, 4%)));
    background: -moz-linear-gradient(top,  darken(@color1, 24%),
darken(@color1, 4%));
    filter:  progid:DXImageTransform.Microsoft.
gradient(startColorstr='darken(@color1, 24%)',
endColorstr='darken(@color1, 4%)');
    }
}
```

7. Let's now tie them all together and set up the namespaces that we will use to style the individual buttons:

```
input.redbutton { #button_base > .button; #button_base >
.medium; .defined_color(#fae7e9); }


input.orangebutton { #button_base > .button; #button_base >
.medium; .defined_color(#fef4e9); }


input.bluebutton { #button_base > .button; #button_base >
.medium; .defined_color(#d9eef7); }
```

8. If all is well, you will see the same as the following screenshot when viewing your work in a browser:

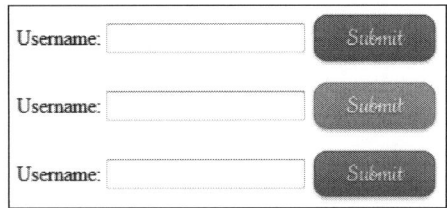

How it works...

In this exercise we've used the power of LESS to group blocks of CSS styles together, thereby reducing the amount of code we need to write; this is very much akin to what most programming languages allow us to do. In this example we've created a base style, which we called `#button_base`. Within this, we've set up two styles: one that controls the button appearance (`.button`) and the other that controls the text appearance (`.medium`). These styles can then be called from the three individual button styles that we are using to create the red, orange, and blue buttons.

This means that if you want to add more styles, you can easily do so; you could for example do something like this:

```
input.greybutton {
    #button_base > .button;
    #button_base > .medium;
    .defined_color(#778899);
}
```

You can then add in an additional button in your HTML code using this style, it will produce the same as the following screenshot:

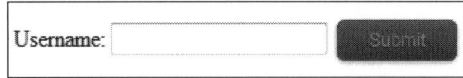

There's more...

While researching for this book, I had originally planned to use a format of code similar to this, to create each of the three buttons as follows:

```
input.redbutton {
    #button_base > .button;
    #button_base > .medium;
    .defined_color(#fae7e9, #b73948, #da5867, #f16c7c, #bf404f,
```

```
#bf404f, #ba4b58, #cf5d6a, #a53845);
}
```

The code worked okay, and served the purpose, but it wasn't the best way to create the buttons. I had to work out which colors to use, and pass through nine individual colors in all to the mixin... surely... I could do better!

I used the darken facility within LESS to work out the colors that should be used, as shown in the following code extract:

```
color: lighten(@color1, 10%);
border: solid 1px darken(@color1, 27%);
background: darken(@color1, 13%);
background: -webkit-gradient(linear, left top, left bottom,
from(darken(@color1, 4%)), to(darken(@color1, 24%)));
```

This means I only need to pass through one color:

```
input.greybutton {
    #button_base > .button;
    #button_base > .medium;
    .defined_color(#778899);
}
```

This surely has to be a better way to code a mixin! You just need to choose a single color to pass through (such as any from `http://html-color-codes.info/color-names/`), and LESS will work out the rest based on your chosen color.

Scoping in LESS (Should know)

If you have spent any time writing programming code, you should already be scoping and using it to control a variable depending on where it has been set in code. Variable scope in LESS is controlled in the same way. Let's take a look at how it works within LESS, using a simple example of styling some `<div>` tags.

Getting ready

This is a simple exercise; all you will need for this one is your text editor.

How to do it...

1. Let's make a start by setting up some basic HTML to demonstrate how scoping works. Create a new document and add a copy of the template code we created at the beginning of this chapter.

2. Add the following inside the `<head>` section:

   ```
   <link rel="stylesheet" type="text/less" href="scoping.less">
   ```

3. Add the following lines of code into the `<body>` section as follows and save it as `test less scoping.html`:

   ```
   <body>
   <div class="item item-1"></div>
   <div class="wrapper w1">
     <div class="item item-1">List Item 1</div>
     <div class="item item-2">List Item 2</div>
   </div>
   <div class="wrapper w2">
     <div class="item item-1">List Item 3</div>
     <div class="item item-2">List Item 4</div>
     <div class="item item-3">List Item 5</div>
     <div class="item item-4">List Item 6</div>
   </div>
   </body>
   ```

4. Go ahead and create a new document; this time save it as `scoping.less` and add the following lines of code, starting with the base variables:

   ```
   //Default Variables
   @width: 98.5%;
   @height: 50px;
   @background: #333;
   @fontcolor: #fff;
   ```

5. We need to add the mixin which will control the base styles for `.item`:

   ```
   .mixin(@width: @width, @height: @height, @background: @background)
   {
     width: @width; height: @height; background: @background;
     float: left; color: @fontcolor; font-weight: bold;
     font: 22px Arial, Helvetica, sans-serif; margin: 3px;    padding:
   5px;
   }

   .item { .mixin(); }
   ```

6. Add the following styles which will override the base mixin:

```
/* Overrides default variables for any .item in the .wrapper div
*/
.wrapper {
    @height: 20px; //Change height
    @background: #360; //Change background color
    .item { .mixin(); }
}
.w1 {
    @width: 48.6%; //Change width
    @background: #854; //Change background color
    padding-top: 10px;
    .item { .mixin(); }
}
.w2 {
    @width: 23.7%; //Change width
    @height: 55px; //Change height
    .item { .mixin(); }
}
```

7. If all is well, you will see something similar to the following screenshot when previewing it in your browser:

How it works...

Remember how we looked at mixins at the start of this book? Well, we've used one here to illustrate scopes in action. If you were to look at the HTML on its own, you might expect the first two `<div>` tags within wrapper w1 to be contained within the `<div>` tag of wrapper w1. However, this won't be the case; the base styles we included in the mixin being used for `.item` are being overridden by additional styles that have been set up for w1 and w2 that override the base wrapper style. We can see the effects of the overridden styles by looking at the compiled CSS from within something like Firebug:

```
/* Uses the Default Mixin */
.item {
    width: 99.5%;
    height: 50px;
    background: #333333;
```

```
    float: left;
    color: #ffffff;
    font-weight: bold;
    font: 22px Arial, Helvetica, sans-serif;
    margin: 3px;
    padding: 5px;
}

/* Overrides default variables for any .item in the .wrapper div */
.wrapper .item {
    width: 99.5%;
    height: 20px;
    background: #336600;
    float: left;
    color: #ffffff;
    font-weight: bold;
    font: 22px Arial, Helvetica, sans-serif;
    margin: 3px;
    padding: 5px;
}

.w1 .item {
    width: 48.6%;
    height: 50px;
    background: #885544;
    float: left;
    color: #ffffff;
    font-weight: bold;
    font: 22px Arial, Helvetica, sans-serif;
    margin: 3px;
    padding: 5px;
}

.w2 .item {
    width: 23.7%;
    height: 55px;
    background: #333333;
    float: left;
    color: #ffffff;
    font-weight: bold;
    font: 22px Arial, Helvetica, sans-serif;
    margin: 3px;
    padding: 5px;
}
```

The downside of using scopes in this manner is that you may get some duplication appear. It just means that you need to take care of which styles are used in the base mixin to help reduce unnecessary duplication.

It's time to move away from theory; we've looked at most parts of the LESS library to see how you can use it to help structure your CSS more effectively. Let's move away from theory, and turn our focus to looking at some real-life examples, beginning with using it to transform some images.

Creating Polaroid effects using LESS (Become an expert)

The well-known Canadian web designer, Nick La, popularized a method of producing a Polaroid effect on some images using CSS3 and some pseudo selectors. You can see his demonstration at `http://webdesignerwall.com/demo/decorative-gallery-2/`. In this recipe we're going to adapt a copy of it to use LESS to achieve the same effect.

Getting ready

For this exercise, you will need to avail yourself of copies of a number of files mentioned as follows:

> - Some of the images from the demo, or copies of your own; for the purpose of this demo, I will assume you have used three images; if you have used different images, please adjust the code accordingly

> - The background and overlay images from the demo on the Web Designer Wall site

> - The mixin library files from `lesselements.com` and `lessprefixer.com`

And yes, you will of course need your text editor!

How to do it...

1. Crank up the normal text editor of your choice, add the following lines of code, and save it as `test less transform.html`:

```
<body>
<ul class="gallery tape transform">
  <li>
    <figure> <a href="#"><img src="images/sample-1.jpg"
alt="image"></a>
       <figcaption>Image Caption</figcaption>
    </figure>
  </li>
```

```
<li>
   <figure> <a href="#"><img src="images/sample-2.jpg"
alt="image"></a>
      <figcaption>Image Caption</figcaption>
   </figure>
  </li>
  <li>
   <figure> <a href="#"><img src="images/sample-3.jpg"
alt="image"></a>
      <figcaption>Image Caption</figcaption>
   </figure>
  </li>
</ul>
</body>
```

2. Add the following lines of code inside the `<head>` section:

```
<title>Demo: Decorative Galleries</title>
<link href='http://fonts.googleapis.com/css?family=Handlee'
rel='stylesheet' type='text/css'>
   <link rel="stylesheet" type="text/less" href="transform.less">
```

3. Let's now add in the LESS code required to style our demo. Create a new document and save it as `transform.less` and add the following code, beginning with the background styles:

```
@import "prefixer.less";
@path: "/images/";

body { background: #fff; color: #666; font: 86%/140% Arial,
Helvetica, sans-serif; width: 800px; max-width: 90%; margin: 0
auto; padding: 20px 0; }
img { border: none; }
p { margin: 0 0 20px; }

a {
   color: #69C; text-decoration: none;

   &:hover { color: #F60; }
}
```

4. Immediately after it, add the following gallery styles:

```
/* based gallery style */
.gallery {
   margin: 0 0 25px; text-align: center;

   li { margin: 5px; list-style: none; display: inline-block; }
```

```
   a { position: relative; display: inline-block; }
}
```

5. We need to add the styles required to position the tape image:

```
/* tape style */
.tape {
   li { width: 170px; padding: 5px; margin: 15px 10px; border:
solid 1px #cac09f; background: #fdf8e4; text-align: center;
      .box-shadow(inset 0 1px rgba(255,255,255,.8), 0 1px 2px
rgba(0,0,0,.2)); }

   figure {
      position: relative; margin: 0;

      &:before { position: absolute; content: ' '; top: 0; left: 0;
width: 100%; height: 100%;
         background: url("@{path}overlay.png") no repeat; }
   }

   figcaption { font: 100%/120% Handlee, Arial, Helvetica, sans-
serif; color: #787568; }

   a:before { position: absolute; z-index: 2; content: ' '; top:
-12px; left: 50%; width: 115px; height: 32px; margin-left: -57px;
      background: url("@{path}tape.png") no-repeat; }
}
```

6. We can then finish by adding in the all-important CSS3 transform effect, which shells out to a transform mixin:

```
.transform {
   background: url("@{path}cork-bg.png"); padding: 25px; border-
radius: 10px; box-shadow: inset 0 1px 5px rgba(0,0,0,.4);

   li { border: none; }
   li:nth-of-type(4n+1) { .transform(rotate(4deg)); }
   li:nth-of-type(2n) { .transform(rotate(-1deg)); }
   li:nth-of-type(4n+3) { .transform(rotate(2deg)); }
}
```

7. If all has goes well, you will see the following in your browser when previewing your results:

How it works...

This recipe illustrates how you can adapt existing code to take advantage of the power of LESS to compile your CSS code. Although we've kept the code close to the original, we've been able to incorporate some useful LESS features:

▶ In the second step we've used string interpolation to create a base folder for our images, so that changing this will update all instances automatically. We're also importing the prefixer and lesselements mixin libraries, ready for use in the code.

▶ In the third and fourth steps we've incorporated nested rules to avoid duplication of style names.

▶ Also in the fourth step we're making a call to the box-shadow mixin that we imported earlier in the recipe. We're also using string interpolation to pull in the overlay and tape images.

▶ In the fifth step we're making two calls: one to the transform mixin in the elements.less library and another to the prefixer.less library for the box-shadow mixin. We're also using the same string interpolation technique you've already seen earlier in this book, which features in the second step of this exercise. This time it is to bring in the cork background image.

There's more...

The original LESS code was written to use a transform mixin available at http://css-tricks.com/snippets/css/useful-css3-less-mixins/, before finding one that had already been included as part of a library of mixins, which is available at http://www.lessprefixer.com.

In this instance either will work perfectly fine, although you may start with one you write manually. Don't be afraid to keep an eye out for existing mixins online; you may find a better option that helps reduce the number of imported files you use!

On the subject of imported files, there is one question we need to answer, which is: Does LESS behave if used with other libraries on the same site or page? Let's take a look at this as part of our next recipe.

Using LESS with other libraries (Become an expert)

As part of using new functionality, web designers or developers will always want to know how well it works with existing functionality. After all, there is no point trying to sell the need to spend lots of money on licensing a package that does everything you need if it doesn't behave well with other software!

In this exercise we're going to take a look at how you could use LESS in conjunction with other packages, using the Modernizr library as our example.

Getting ready

For this exercise all you will need is your trusty text editor, a photo (preferably in PNG format), and a copy of the `elements.less` mixin you downloaded earlier in this chapter. It doesn't matter what the subject of the photo is, I will assume for the purpose of this recipe that it is called `photo.png` and is 200 px by 300 px in size. I've used the spiral staircase image available from `http://pixabay.com/en/spiral-staircase-stairs-58328/`, and have resized it accordingly.

How to do it...

1. Crack open the text editor of your choice, add the following lines of code to a new document, and save it as `test less compatibility.html`:

```
<!DOCTYPE html>
<html lang="en" dir="ltr" id="ala-modernizr-sample" class="no-js">
<head>
  <meta charset="utf-8">
  <title>My Beautiful Sample Page</title>
  <link href='http://fonts.googleapis.com/css?family=Devonshire'
rel='stylesheet' type='text/css'>
  <link rel="stylesheet" type="text/css" href="styles.css"
media="screen">
  <link rel="stylesheet/less" type="text/css" href="compatibility.
less">
```

```
    <script type="text/javascript" src="http://cdnjs.cloudflare.com/
ajax/libs/less.js/1.3.1/less.min.js"></script>
    <script src="http://cdnjs.cloudflare.com/ajax/libs/
modernizr/2.6.2/modernizr.min.js"></script>
</head>
<body>
    <div id="content">
        <h1>My Beautiful Sample Page</h1>
        <p>Lorem ipsum dolor sit amet, consectetur adipiscing elit.
Morbi eleifend sem id ipsum luctus eu semper quam lacinia. Nunc ut
arcu non sapien adipiscing scelerisque non vel quam. Ut porttitor,
augue nec suscipit congue, turpis nulla faucibus enim, sit amet
consectetur erat enim vitae dolor.</p>
        <section>
            <h2>Modernizr</h2>
            <p>Ut sed arcu at tortor ornare pulvinar vel nec nisl. Cras
venenatis tortor turpis, eu pulvinar enim. Aenean eget lorem mi.
Aenean malesuada fermentum lobortis. Vestibulum vulputate tortor
nisi, elementum tincidunt libero. Fusce et massa id dui tristique
mollis eu consequat urna.</p>
            <img src="photo.png" width="200" height="300" alt="Photo of
steps">
        </section>
        <p>This is a random list:</p>
        <ol>
            <li>Lorem ipsum dolor sit amet, consectetur adipiscing
elit.</li>
            <li>Aenean congue condimentum risus, id mattis magna
tincidunt at.</li>
            <li>Mauris sollicitudin nunc a nibh tempor ac interdum
diam iaculis.</li>
            <li>Nunc pharetra mauris eget mi congue pellentesque.</li>
            <li>Ut ac nulla mi, in tincidunt neque.</li>
        </ol>
    </div>
    <footer>This is a test</footer></body>
</html>
```

2. Create a new blank document, add the following lines of code, and save it as
   `compatibility.less`. Make sure you have your copy of `elements.less`
   in the same folder as your exercise files:

```less
@import "elements.less";
@activelink: #e33a89;
@linkcolor: #941350;

.boxshadow section img { .box-shadow(0 0 3px #000); }
```

```
.csstransforms section img { position: relative; top: 20px;
.rotation(5deg); }
.boxshadow #content { border: none; .box-shadow(3px 3px 6px
rgba(0,0,0, .5)); }
.borderradius #content { .rounded(12px); }

a {
  &:link { color: @linkcolor; font-weight: bold; }
  &:visited { color: @linkcolor; font-weight: bold; }
  &:focus { color: @activelink; text-decoration: none; }
  &:hover { color: @activelink; text-decoration: none; }
}
#content h1+p {
  margin: 20px 0;
  &:first-line { font-weight: bold; font-variant: small-caps; }
}

.no-csscolumns ol.features {
  float: left;
  margin: 0 0 20px;
  li { float: left; width: 180px; }
}

.js section {
  float: none; position: absolute; right: 40px; top: 40px;
  p { font-size: 11px; line-height: 16px; }
  h1 { line-height: 50px; }
}

section {
  float: right; text-align: justify; width: 200px; }
  h2 { margin: 0; height: 70px; text-indent: -9999px; width:
200px; }
  p, li { font-size: 12px; line-height: 16px; margin: 0 0 30px;
padding: 0 30px 0 0; width: 200px; }
}
```

3. We need to add some more styles, create a new document, add the following lines of code, and save it as `styles.css`:

```
body { -webkit-text-stroke:1px transparent; }
@media only screen and (max-device-width:480px) {body{-webkit-
text-stroke:0 black;}}

html, body { background: #5a71a0; color: #141414; font: normal
14px/20px Helvetica, Verdana, Arial, sans-serif;
```

```
      margin: 0; padding: 0; text-align: center; }

  img { vertical-align: bottom; }
  #content { background: #fafafa; border: 2px outset #666; margin:
  20px auto 10px; padding: 40px 40px 20px;
    text-align: left; width: 500px; }

  h1 { color: #2e384d; font: 37px/37px 'Devonshire'; margin: 0;
  text-shadow: #aaa 5px 5px 5px; }

  ol.features { font-size: 12px; line-height: 18px; list-style:
  none; margin: 0; padding: 0; }

  footer {
    font-size: 11px; font-style: oblique;
    a { font-style: normal; }
  }

  .js #content { padding-right: 280px; position: relative; width:
  290px; }

  .rgba h1 { text-shadow: ) 5px 5px 5px rgba(148,19,80, .3; }
  @font-face { src: url(Beautiful-ES.ttf); font-family:
  'Beautiful'; }

  .fontface h1 { font: 42px/50px 'Devonshire'; margin: 0; text-
  shadow: none; }

  .csscolumns ol.features {
    columns: 2;
    -o-columns: 2;
    -moz-column-count: 2;
    -webkit-columns: 2;
  }
```

4. If you preview the results in your browser, you will see something like the following screenshot:

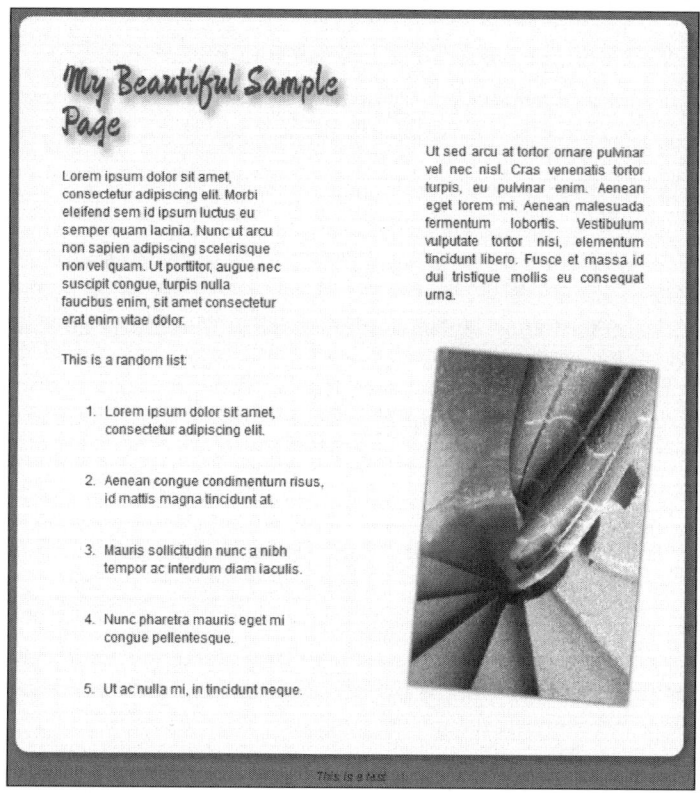

How it works...

In this recipe I've used a demo created by Faruk Ates, which shows how to incorporate Modernizr into your site (if you want to see the original, it's available at http://www.alistapart.com/d/taking-advantage-of-html5-and-css3-with-modernizr/sample-medium.html), and I've reworked it to use LESS to build the CSS dynamically.

If you've not used Modernizr before, then key to Modernizr is its ability to work out if it supports a particular feature, and not the version of the browser being used. The latter is open to being unreliable. It inserts CSS styles which are then used to indicate if a feature is supported; it adds a no- tag to each style if it is not supported in your browser.

In our recipe I've converted a number of styles into LESS equivalents and hived them off to a separate file in our code; keeping them in the same stylesheet as the other CSS styles would have confused Modernizr and LESS. If you look closely at the compiled code in something like Firebug, you will see there are some styles there for features that are not supported, such as `no-cssreflections`. For those styles that are required, but are not supported, fallback styles have been included in the CSS and/or LESS files. If you want to see the difference, try viewing the same page within Firefox and IE and you will see a real difference!

There's more...

The beauty of LESS is that it creates standard CSS styles when compiled. This means that it could be used in a variety of environments; if it doesn't work, or the site is too big, when used dynamically, you can always precompile the code using something like Crunch and add the resulting CSS files manually. There is an array of other libraries which could be used with LESS. To whet your appetite, here are a few:

- **Yepnope.js** (`http://www.yepnopejs.com`): This is often used with Modernizr; it's a basic way to determine support for a feature in your browser and decide whether to use the normal support or a fallback version.

- **Prefixr.com** (`http://www.prefixr.com`): Although there are mixins available to support most of what is offered by this site (such as `http://css-tricks.com/snippets/css/useful-css3-less-mixins/`), you could still use it to ensure mixins are kept up-to-date with changing styles.

- **320 and Up**: This is billed as the *tiny screen first responsive boilerplate*; this uses LESS mixins to help reduce the style code required within the system. It's available at `http://stuffandnonsense.co.uk/projects/320andup/`.

- **Bootstrap**: This is available at `https://github.com/twitter/bootstrap`; it's a frontend toolkit which contains a number of user interface components and interactions. It uses LESS extensively, principally in the form of mixins that are available for use in the library.

- **Respond.js**: This polyfill library is available to download from `https://github.com/scottjehl/Respond/`, and provides CSS3-based media enquiry support for browsers that don't support them by default as part of building responsive sites. You may have to compile your LESS code first before including the `Respond.js` library.

- **Fraction.less**: This is a boilerplate system available at `http://fractionless.info/`; it was based on HTML5 Boilerplate but adds support for LESS while removing some of the bloat from the original version.

- **Node.js**: We've already touched on this earlier in this chapter briefly; Node.js (available from `http://www.nodejs.org`), is perfect as part of adding support for LESS and other libraries to text editors such as Sublime Text 2 (`http://www.sublimetext.com`) or Notepad++ (`http://www.notepad-plus-plus.org/`).

There are plenty more available online—happy hunting! In the meantime, let's turn our focus to using prebuilt mixin libraries and see how you can use these within your code as part of the next recipe.

Using pre-built mixin libraries (Become an expert)

Throughout this book we've looked at how you can write code more efficiently by using the LESS library. In particular, we've covered how you can create your own mixins, which will help save you time when writing code, particularly if it involves adding vendor prefixes! You could spend time writing these mixins, and this will surely be a valuable exercise, but it will take time that could be better spent elsewhere. Instead, why not have a look online to see if a mixin has already been written. Lots of people have written their own mixin libraries over time, and this could save you a lot of unnecessary work.

In this final recipe we're going to look at how you can use one such mixin library to create some progress bars. The code we will use is based on some I found posted at CSS Deck (`http://www.cssdeck.com`), which we will adapt to use with the mixin library at `http://www.lesselements.com`.

Getting ready

For this exercise you will need to avail yourself of a copy of the mixin from `http://www.lesselements.com`; the download file is available at `https://github.com/dmitryf/elements/zipball/master`. Other than this, all you will need is your normal text editor.

How to do it...

1. Crank up your normal text editor, create a new document and add the following code, and save it as `test less progressbar.html`:

```
<!DOCType html>
<html>
  <head>
    <link href='http://fonts.googleapis.com/css?family=Cookie'
rel='stylesheet' type='text/css'>
    <link rel="stylesheet/less" type="text/css" href="progressbar.
less">
    <script src="http://lesscss.googlecode.com/files/less-1.3.0.min.
js"></script>
  </head>
<body>
<div class="green progressbar"></div>
<div class="blue progressbar" style="width: 125px;"></div>
```

```html
<div class="red progressbar" style="width: 62.5px;"></div>
<div class="progressbar" style="width: 31.25px;"></div>
</body>
</html>
```

2. Create a second new document, add the following LESS code, and save it as `progressbar.less`. There is a fair bit of code, so we will go through it section by section, beginning with the imports:

```less
@import "elements";
@import "mixins";

body { background-color:#4C4C4C; }
```

3. We add the base LESS style for the progress bar. This uses two mixins: one of which is from `lesselements.com`, and the other is my own:

```less
.progressbar { margin:25px; width:250px; height:20px;
    .border-radius(6px, 6px, 6px, 6px);
    .box-shadow(inset 0px 0px 5px rgba(255,255,255,0.5));
    position: relative;
    -webkit-animation: progress 2s 1 forwards;
    -moz-animation: progress 2s 1 forwards;
    -ms-animation: progress 2s 1 forwards;
    animation: progress 2s 1 forwards;
}
```

4. Although the basic progress bar style is now defined, it's not going to look very stylish just yet, so let's fix that by adding in some more styles:

```less
.progressbar::after { content: '';
    margin: 0;
    padding: 0;
    width: 100%;
    height: 100%;
    position: absolute;
    top: 0;
    left: 0;
    .linear-b-gradient(-45deg, transparent, transparent 8.5px,
rgba(255,255,255,.2) 1px, rgba(255,255,255,.2) 17px);
}
```

5. The last part of the LESS styling is to give each progress bar its own colors. In this instance we're using red, green, and blue; the code shells outputs to one of my own mixins:

```less
.blue { .gradient(top, rgba(109,179,242,1) 0%, rgba(84,163,238,1)
50%, rgba(54,144,240,1) 51%, rgba(30,105,222,1) 100%); }
.green { .gradient(top, rgba(157,213,58,1) 0%,rgba(161,213,79,1)
```

```
50%,rgba(128,194,23,1) 51%,rgba(124,188,10,1) 100%); }
.red { .gradient(top, rgba(248,80,50,1) 0%,rgba(248,80,50,1)
50%,rgba(246,41,12,1) 51%,rgba(231,56,39,1) 100%); }
```

```
@-webkit-keyframes progress { from {} to {width: 400px;} }
@-moz-keyframes progress { from {} to {width: 400px;} }
@-ms-keyframes progress { from {} to {width: 400px;} }
@keyframes progress { from {} to {width: 400px;} }
```

6. The last step is to add the code for two mixins that are being referenced: one using the `linear-gradient` style and the other for `repeating-linear-gradient`:

```
.gradient(@o: top, @s: #fff, @e: #cccccc, @t: #ffc, @f: #ccc ) {
  background: -webkit-linear-gradient(@o, @s, @e, @t, @f);
  background: -moz-linear-gradient(@o, @s, @e, @t, @f);
  background: -ms-linear-gradient(@o, @s, @e, @t, @f);
  background: -o-linear-gradient(@o, @s, @e, @t, @f);
  background: linear-gradient(@o, @s, @e, @t, @f);
}
```

```
.linear-b-gradient(@p1: -45deg, @p2: transparent, @p3:
transparent 8.5px, @color1: rgba(255,255,255,.2) 1px, @color2:
rgba(255,255,255,.2) 17px) {
  background: -webkit-repeating-linear-gradient(@p1, @p2, @p3,
@color1, @color2);
  background: -moz-repeating-linear-gradient(@p1, @p2, @p3,
@color1, @color2);
  background: -ms-repeating-linear-gradient(@p1, @p2, @p3,
@color1, @color2);
  background: -o-repeating-linear-gradient(@p1, @p2, @p3, @color1,
@color2);
  background: repeating-linear-gradient(@p1, @p2, @p3, @color1,
@color2);
}
```

7. If all is well, you will see the following in your browser when viewing the results:

How it works...

Although the code in the LESS stylesheet may look complicated, in reality it is simpler than it looks; mixins work in a similar fashion as that of functions in most programming languages.

In this instance we've provided calls to four mixins in all; two are being referenced from the prebuilt mixin library from `lesselements.com`, and two reference my own LESS mixin file. In all cases we pass through a number of different variables, which LESS then substitutes in to the placeholders within each mixin. A key point not to forget is that although we've included more mixins than have actually been used, LESS will only include those that have been referenced from our style code, which in this instance will be `.box-shadow` and `.border-radius`, in addition to the other two that are being used.

There's more...

It is well worth doing research online to see if others have created any mixins that fit in with your requirements; there are hundreds of people who have created or contributed to mixins, either as individual ones or as part of a library.

To get you started, here are some you may want to look at for using within your projects:

- **LESS Elements**: `http://www.lesselements.com`
- **LESS Hat**: `http://lesshat.com/`
- **Adding vendor prefixes to LESS styles**: `http://www.lessprefixer.com/`
- **Some example mixins you should use**: `http://designshack.net/articles/css/10-less-css-examples-you-should-steal-for-your-projects/`
- **CSS3Please.less Mixins, from Greg Babula**: `http://coderwall.com/p/alumra`

There are plenty more available for you to try; you can pick whichever you prefer to use that fits your requirements, or perhaps create your own library!

Thank you for buying
Instant LESS CSS Preprocessor How-to

About Packt Publishing

Packt, pronounced 'packed', published its first book "*Mastering phpMyAdmin for Effective MySQL Management*" in April 2004 and subsequently continued to specialize in publishing highly focused books on specific technologies and solutions.

Our books and publications share the experiences of your fellow IT professionals in adapting and customizing today's systems, applications, and frameworks. Our solution based books give you the knowledge and power to customize the software and technologies you're using to get the job done. Packt books are more specific and less general than the IT books you have seen in the past. Our unique business model allows us to bring you more focused information, giving you more of what you need to know, and less of what you don't.

Packt is a modern, yet unique publishing company, which focuses on producing quality, cutting-edge books for communities of developers, administrators, and newbies alike. For more information, please visit our website: www.packtpub.com.

Writing for Packt

We welcome all inquiries from people who are interested in authoring. Book proposals should be sent to author@packtpub.com. If your book idea is still at an early stage and you would like to discuss it first before writing a formal book proposal, contact us; one of our commissioning editors will get in touch with you.

We're not just looking for published authors; if you have strong technical skills but no writing experience, our experienced editors can help you develop a writing career, or simply get some additional reward for your expertise.

Ext JS 4 Web Application Development Cookbook

ISBN: 978-1-84951-686-0   Paperback: 488 pages

Over 110 easy-to-follow recipes backed up with real-life examples, walking you through basic Ext JS features to advanced application design using Sencha Ext JS

1. Learn how to build Rich Internet Applications with the latest version of the Ext JS framework in a cookbook style

2. From creating forms to theming your interface, you will learn the building blocks for developing the perfect web application

3. Easy to follow recipes step through practical and detailed examples which are all fully backed up with code, illustrations, and tips

HTML5 Canvas Cookbook

ISBN: 978-1-84969-136-9   Paperback: 348 pages

Over 80 recipes to revolutionize the web experience with HTML5 Canvas

1. The quickest way to get up to speed with HTML5 Canvas application and game development

2. Create stunning 3D visualizations and games without Flash

3. Written in a modern, unobtrusive, and objected oriented JavaScript style so that the code can be reused in your own applications.

Please check **www.PacktPub.com** for information on our titles

HTML5 Video How-To

ISBN: 978-1-84969-364-6

Over 20 practical, hands-on recipes to encode and display videos in the HTML5 video standard

1. Learn something new in an Instant! A short, fast, focused guide delivering immediate results.

2. Encode and embed videos into web pages using the HTML5 video standard

3. Publish videos to popular sites, such as YouTube or VideoBinl

Responsive Web Design with HTML5 and CSS3

ISBN: 978-1-84969-318-9   Paperback: 324 pages

Learn responsive design using HTML5 and CSS3 to adapt websites to any browser or screen size

1. Everything needed to code websites in HTML5 and CSS3 that are responsive to every device or screen size

2. Learn the main new features of HTML5 and use CSS3's stunning new capabilities including animations, transitions and transformations

3. Real world examples show how to progressively enhance a responsive design while providing fall backs for older browsers

Please check **www.PacktPub.com** for information on our titles

Printed in Great Britain
by Amazon.co.uk, Ltd.,
Marston Gate.